"If you take *Limitless* seriously it will c̶h̶a̶n̶g̶e̶ ̶y̶o̶u̶r̶ ̶l̶i̶f̶e̶ ̶f̶o̶r̶e̶v̶e̶r̶.̶ ̶P̶e̶t̶e̶ story is inspiring and authentic, and in the pages you now hold he lays out a practical blueprint to his success. Read it slowly. Do the exercises. The chapter on mentoring alone is worth the read. In fact, I've wanted many people in my life to be mentored by Pete Ruppert. Now with this book they finally can be."

— **Jason Jaggard**, Executive Coach and Founding Partner of Novus Global and The Institute for Meta Performance

"Pete Ruppert is a lifelong learner and an inspiring teacher. His book *Limitless* is packed with fascinating stories and practical tools to help you think differently and make a bigger impact. Buy it. Read it. Implement it. It could change your life."

— **Ryan Hawk**, host of *The Learning Leader Show* and author of *Welcome to Management*

"By sharing his own stories and being vulnerable, Pete Ruppert effectively reminds us that the path to success is not a straight line. I wish I had read this book when I was getting my start!"

— **James Keane**, President and CEO, Steelcase

"*Limitless* comes at a perfect time for those who don't want to settle for 'good enough.' In today's uncertain world, this book provides a simple but powerful guide to actually creating a unique and extraordinary life. I've personally observed these attributes in many successful people I've worked with over the years—from entrepreneurs, to entertainers, to athletes. If you're trying to get ahead or re-start, this is a must read guide to achieving your dreams."

— **Verne Harnish**, Founder of Entrepreneurs' Organization (EO) and author of *Scaling Up (Rockefeller Habits 2.0)*

LIMITLESS

LIMITLESS

NINE STEPS

TO LAUNCH YOUR ONE
EXTRAORDINARY LIFE

PETER G. RUPPERT

credo
house publishers

To my late parents

To my dad, my original and greatest mentor.
He taught me the importance of integrity,
hard work and doing things right. He also helped
launch my entrepreneurial journey by loaning me
the money to buy a tractor for my first business:
a lawn mowing company.

And to my mom, an encourager who always saw
the good in everyone she met. Her deep faith,
love for life and acceptance of others were great
examples to me and to the rest of my family.

CONTENTS

It is not the critic who counts; not the man who points out how the strong man stumbles, or where the doer of deeds could have done them better.

The credit belongs to the man who is actually in the arena, whose face is marred by dust and sweat and blood;

who strives valiantly; who errs, who comes up short again and again, because there is no effort without error and shortcoming; but who does actually strive to do the deeds;

who knows great enthusiasms, the great devotions; who spends himself in a worthy cause;

who at the best knows in the end the triumph of high achievement, and who at the worst, if he fails, at least fails while daring greatly, so that his place shall never be with those cold and timid souls who know neither victory nor defeat.

—THEODORE ROOSEVELT

INTRODUCTION

Consider the difference between limitless living—living boldly, loving what we do and achieving our dreams—and limited living—being frustrated, marginally happy and unfulfilled. Why is it that some people are able to achieve huge successes while others drift from day to day? How do some, despite extremely challenging circumstances, rise up to make a big impact or achieve great things and others, given the benefit of significant talent or opportunity, end up settling for so much less? What makes the difference?

This book was written for those, young and old, who want something more in their lives, who have big goals, who aren't satisfied with their current situation. They simply don't want to settle for the status quo or for "good enough" and have dreams they want to chase, not give up on.

Throughout the course of our lives, we will all face a multitude of challenges. We will struggle with self-doubt. We will experience career and even personal failures. During these times, it's important to know that we're not alone and that others have been in similar situations and have still found their way to create a great life and successful career they love.

How do I know this? Because my own life has followed a similar path. I've experienced my share of failures along with successes, and I'm excited to share the lessons and principles I've learned along the way.

It was during my own times of failure and disappointment that I first began to study what made other people successful in work and life, and, over time, I found nine common themes almost universally present in extraordinary people. I first captured them as a list to guide my own actions on my personal journey. I later placed the list on my kids' bathroom mirror to be a constant reminder to them. I even laminated it and titled it "Traits of a Champion" with the hope it would inspire them to always strive for their best and never give up, even when they fail. All four of my kids have grown up seeing these nine traits every day when they get up and before they go to bed.

Eventually, I began sharing the list with others: first at a conference and then at subsequent speaking events and talks with my team and other young adults. These talks generated so much interest in the nine common themes that I decided to summarize my thoughts and experiences and capture them in this book. My goal in writing it has been to share what I've learned and to help shorten the learning curve for others who are looking for more and want the same kind of inspiration and guidance.

Finding and learning to integrate these traits into my daily activities has not only helped change the trajectory of my own life—I've also seen it do the same for others. My wish is that it will have the same impact for my children and for everyone who reads this book.

Throughout its pages, I hope this book communicates that each one of us is born with a unique combination of talent, skills and smarts that, when put to concerted use, can allow us to create the kind of limitless life we imagine.

Every one of us has the potential to serve the world in our own unique way. No matter the situation, the frustrations or the difficulties we've faced, it's possible to overcome and pursue our dreams. It is our choice. It is up to us. We don't have to just live from one day to the next. We can control our destiny and can progress toward creating the life we envision.

It is never too early or too late to start. It takes some careful planning and intentionality, but a proactive, consistent approach will ultimately lead us to where we hope to be.

When I first read President Theodore Roosevelt's words at the beginning of this introduction, I was captivated. It's my favorite quote of all time and has been a constant reminder for me. The key to success in work and life is more than arriving in the world with our specific talents and abilities and expecting things to just work out—it's about actually getting into the arena and doing the work. It's about standing up and fighting hard, every day, for what we hope to achieve. It's about struggling and failing. And then getting back up, again and again.

This journey of ups and downs, of wins and losses, is typical of what virtually every successful person has experienced. There are no overnight success stories. In researching successful individuals, I have learned that there's no substitute for hard work and that even the most successful people in the world struggle with self-doubt. We all face fatigue, discouragement and disappointment along the way. Every one of us has our own journey and learning curve.

Whether you're just finishing school and ready to attack the world or are mid-career and looking for inspiration or to make a change, my hope is that these nine steps can become the foundational building blocks to inspire you to cast your own vision, follow your own dreams and do the work to create your one extraordinary life.

Pete

All that we are is the result of what we have thought.
The mind is everything. What we think, we shall become.

—BUDDHA

The secret of change is to focus all of your energy,
not on fighting the old, but on building the new.

—DAN MILLMAN

And if I asked you to name all the things that you love,
how long would it take for you to name yourself?

—ANONYMOUS

CHAPTER 1

WIN THE BATTLE IN YOUR HEAD

PERSPECTIVE MATTERS

Early in my eighth-grade year, my dad suggested that I attend a large, all-boys high school across town from where we lived. Although I definitely wasn't excited at first—especially at the prospect of leaving my friends and not having girls in my school—he left the final choice up to me. Ultimately, I decided to go, largely because the all-boys school had a highly successful basketball program and basketball was my favorite sport.

In an ironic twist, I got cut from the basketball team that first year. I was extremely disappointed and lost. I seriously considered going back to my previous school where I knew I already fit in and could easily make the team. That would have been the simple and easy route. But I also wondered if I could dig deep and overcome this obstacle. Was I going to believe that I wasn't good enough to compete at my new school? Or, could I find a way to dig deeper, work hard and make the team next season?

We all experience positive and negative self-talk like this on a regular basis. Whether you realize it or not, you're probably having the same internal conversations over and over every day. These two opposing voices compete for our mindset every day and every minute.

For example, when something bad or disappointing happens, we can easily be swayed by our negative self-talk. We all know this voice well. It's the one that told me I wasn't good enough to make the basketball team my freshman year. That negative voice told me things like: *You're a failure. Life isn't fair. Stretching yourself is too risky.*

On the other hand, there's a positive voice that can join our internal dialog. It encourages us to focus on the good aspects of every situation, chalking up the negative ones to learning opportunities. When we decide to listen to this voice, we refuse to let our bad experiences define us and bring us down, and we're encouraged to wonder what we can learn from the situation. Focusing on the positive can help us grow to become even better despite our challenges.

When I listened to this positive voice during my freshman year of high school, I imagined not giving up, working hard all summer to improve my basketball game and eventually making the team my sophomore year.

I've learned that these internal conversations are crucial to the success or failure of everything I do, large and small, from my business ventures to my daily activities. The internal dialogue I have with myself—and whether it's largely positive or negative—has played a pivotal role in my ability (or inability) to overcome difficulties and achieve success in life and work.

The reason is simple: when I let the negative self-talk win more often than the positive self-talk, I begin to allow my bad experiences to define my future. I can develop a pattern of being afraid to take risks in both big and small decisions, if I'm not careful. When I let the negative experiences I've had define and drive me, I lose confidence—and more importantly, I lose hope.

On the flipside, the world is full of examples of others who have gone through enormous trials and somehow maintained enough faith in themselves to eventually experience incredible success.

Why do some people rebound and find success while others shrink away from working hard to achieve their dreams and goals? The difference is this: those who succeed have worked to allow positive self-talk to triumph over negative. They have won the "battle in their head" by not allowing their negative thoughts (which are always present) to drown out the positive. They have refused to let bad experiences define or drive them. Instead, they have turned those experiences into learning opportunities.

Do you listen more often to positive or negative thoughts? How might your future look different if you actively seek out positive perspectives on your situation and reframe the negative thoughts to become more positive?

This is exactly what I finally chose to do when it came to playing basketball during my sophomore year. I decided to believe anything was possible, and then I put in the long hours that entire summer to become a better player. I certainly knew there was a chance I would fail again, but I decided to try anyway. I decided to believe I could become good enough.

And sure enough, my sophomore year came, and the belief in myself and the extra dedication paid off and I made the team. I didn't play much, but I kept working hard, and as a junior I made the varsity team. Then, in my senior year I was elected captain by my teammates. This was one of my first experiences where I learned the vital importance of winning the battle in my head. It was a crucial learning moment for me and a foundational experience that I later was able to draw upon, time and time again, when facing even more difficult challenges.

WHICH LENS DO YOU USE?

One of the most important lessons we can learn in life is that we always have the ability to choose which voice we listen to. Each one of us gets to choose whether we want to have a positive or a negative outlook on ourselves and our future. No one else gets to decide this for us. We ultimately make this choice. It is up to us.

Carol Dweck, author of *Mindset: The New Psychology of Success*, says we all go through life with one of two dominant mindsets: a growth mindset or a fixed mindset.

People with a **fixed mindset** believe that their talents and skills are fixed and don't really change over time. Those with this mindset focus on doing only what they believe they can do well and accomplish successfully. They usually think their worth resides in their successes, so they tend to play it safe, rather than challenging themselves, taking risks and potentially risking failure. They are often paralyzed when it comes to taking action, especially if the action or activity seems risky. Because of this, they usually choose opportunities that seem "doable" over those

> Are you winning the battle in your head? What steps can you take to ensure that the positive inclinations win out more than the negative ones?

that stretch them and help them grow. They also worry about being judged, and they easily see failure as a setback, rather than a learning or growth opportunity. Those with a fixed mindset choose to let their negative voices dominate their thoughts. They tend to stay in a "safe zone."

Those with a **growth mindset** believe the opposite. They know that with focus and effort, they can improve their intelligence, skills and talents. Success for those with a growth mindset comes about as they focus on stretching and developing themselves. Their passion for stretching themselves, even when things are not going well, is a hallmark of this mindset and allows them to thrive even in the most challenging times of their life. This is because those with a growth mindset see every failure as a potential learning opportunity, rather than a devastating and permanent setback. Because of this, they prioritize learning and growth opportunities. They embrace opportunities to get better and smarter. Those who consistently foster a growth mindset embrace their positive voices, even in tough times.

IT'S YOUR CHOICE

Whether your current mindset is more fixed or tends more toward growth, it doesn't matter. The important thing for each of us to realize is that we have options, and we *can* change our mindset. We have the ability to set the tone for ourselves and get to decide whether the positive conversations in our head get to speak louder than the negative ones.

Starting our career and life with a positive mindset can be a game changer. According to Dweck, the view we adopt for ourselves profoundly affects the way we lead our life. "It can determine whether you become the person you want to be and whether you accomplish the things you value."

It's tough to win in life until you win the battle with yourself. And the first step begins with realizing you have a choice. You can actually choose to win the battle in your head. Training yourself to do so starts with each decision you make during the course of a day—from the smallest to the largest ones.

PRACTICAL STEPS TOWARD A POSITIVE MINDSET

1. Choose positivity

Realize that awareness and choosing to practice a positive mindset is the first and most important step to future success. We have to understand and deeply internalize that winning the battle in our head is the most important thing we can do (which is why we're discussing it in chapter 1). Winning here is where it all starts. You have to believe in yourself first.

2. List positive thoughts

Begin to build a list of your personal accomplishments and positive traits. No matter how much we struggle or how often we let negative thoughts speak too loudly, it's important to also remember the accomplishments that have made us proud and the personal characteristics that have helped us along our journey. It will be helpful to remind yourself of this by writing it all down and revisiting your notes regularly.

3. Learn the art of reframing

Every time you start thinking negative or unhelpful thoughts, catch yourself. Become aware of the thought and introduce a counter argument that can reframe it into something more positive. For example, reframe the thought, "I'm a terrible public speaker," into, "With a bit of practice, I bet I can grow into a better public speaker." Once you become more aware of these patterns and proactively address them in the moment, you will slowly start to change.

4. Realize you're not alone

Accept that EVERYONE has had their own self-doubts and everyone has failed . . . a lot! Don't let failure define you (we'll talk a lot more about this in chapter 6). Too often, we think only we experience failure or have weaknesses. But *everyone* has failed. The key is how we respond to these failures.

5. Don't let the past define you

This is a choice everyone can make. Only you can allow the negativity of your past experiences, relationships and treatment by others to define your future. Your brighter future starts right now if you choose to reframe. By choosing not to allow your past to darken your future, you can begin to see and create the life you dream about. Let this be the mindset that drives you forward into the future.

6. Dwell on your daily victories

At the end of every day, write down three things that went well (your "victories"). Keep a log. Fill your mind with those positive thoughts and beliefs. The more you do this, the more you'll see change.

Ultimately, winning the battle in your head results in self-confidence. If you allow it, this self-confidence builds on itself and will carry you leaps and bounds into the future.

MY STORY

A Tale of Two Futures: Version 1

In 1991, I was close to graduating from Harvard Business School and ready to conquer the world, so I started a side business. That side business took off, and a year later, when it became too big to handle on top of my new day job, I sold it and generated a significant profit.

About that same time—less than a year into my new career at a successful consulting firm—my boss came to me and said, "You and I can do this better. Let's start our own consulting firm."

As an excited "entrepreneur-to-be," I jumped at the opportunity to start a new venture at age twenty-eight. I was excited and felt prepared. Within five years, the firm grew to four offices across the Eastern US., and I sold the company, again making a strong return.

Then, wanting to get out of the consulting industry and looking to find a high-potential company with big growth prospects, I landed a position as president of a small education company. I moved my family and led the company as it grew from four schools to fifty-one schools in eight years.

After success at this company, I was recruited to run a healthcare company—a "too good to be true opportunity" with big financial returns that I couldn't turn down. As CEO, I quickly helped the company achieve greater success, and many perks followed.

Wanting to get back into education, I then decided to raise money to start a company that would acquire and replicate successful private schools. Given previous successes and what I believed to be a well-conceived plan, I quickly raised the money. The new company started acquiring schools, we found a successful model to replicate and then grew quickly from there over the next several years, making the company a strong example of success by almost any measure.

A Tale of Two Futures: Version 2

I started the same side hustle mentioned previously while in business school, but it crashed and burned, and I lost all the money I put into it. The consulting firm I started did reach four offices and had some nice growth and success, but it was never properly capitalized, so it was always short on cash.

Five years later, with the weight of four offices, a larger payroll and a sudden drop in revenues, my partner and I ran out of cash. We had to let everyone go, shut down the business and restart as independent consultants. By age thirty-two, I had started two businesses, and both had failed. My first child was on the way, and I was unemployed.

After working independently as a consultant for a while, I was eventually offered a job as president of a small education company. Under my leadership, the company found great success, but over time I became impatient, frustrated and made a rash decision to accept an opportunity with a healthcare company that seemed exciting, offered me more money and allowed me to finally be a CEO.

That healthcare company turned out to indeed be "too good to be true." I had not done enough homework and didn't get all the facts. I was enamored with the owner's private jets and helicopter, along with the promised upside potential, which I never got in writing before I started. In reality, it was a disaster for me, and I resigned only six months into the role with no immediate job prospects and no pay. Again, I was unemployed—this time with a fourth child on the way.

Raising money to start an education company wasn't actually so quick, and it took twelve months and at least fifty pitches (forty-seven of which ended in a "no").

The company experienced anything but a rapid rise to success. There were more losses than wins in the early years. After just twelve months, a large investor representing fifty percent of our capital completely pulled their financial commitment because they didn't believe the company had a winning strategy. Every single school the company acquired during those early years saw results drop after its acquisition. The board wasn't happy, tensions were high, and the company was off to a rocky start.

A Tale of Two Futures: The Real Story

Both versions are about me—but version 1 is almost entirely false. It's a romanticized, "storybook" summary that many who don't know me might believe.

Version 2 is what *actually* happened.

Today Fusion Education Group provides a powerful educational experience for thousands of kids per year and is a special company with amazing people, teachers and leaders that are committed to our mission.

But several times the "car" almost crashed.

In retrospect, I'm thankful for those misses and near crashes. The failures magnified my weaknesses and made me come to grips with them. My impatience, my tendency to brush over important details, my naïve optimism, my relative inexperience as a younger leader and my fear of asking for help all led directly or indirectly to the mistakes I made.

But the misses and failures also saved me. They helped me improve. They forced me to rethink what I needed to do to be successful. They were an important part of my story. I embrace them, and I'm thankful for them every day.

As I've learned and grown, I can see how mindset has played a crucial role in my journey.

- At twenty-seven, I was a hotshot business school graduate.
- At thirty-two, I was unemployed with a family and a child on the way.
- At forty-three, I was unemployed again.

I was embarrassed each time, and I had to do a lot of soul-searching to find my way. I had my share of negative voices telling me I was a failure. Had I chosen to let those negative voices win, who knows where I'd be today.

Thankfully, I chose to listen to the positive voices that told me failure didn't have to define me. I could get back up and still pursue my dreams. My ability to win that conversation with myself—by choosing a positive mindset—is what helped me refocus on my passion, learn from my experiences and get back up into life's arena. It allowed me to move forward and create a positive and successful future.

I assembled the list of nine traits you'll find in this book during a very dark time for me as I was trying my best to find my way. Today, I carry them in my briefcase wherever I go. I also taped them on my kids' bathroom mirror, and I hope they've also learned from them. These nine traits are actually quite simple, but they've carried me through all my challenges and all that I've learned so far.

I never turned back. I never gave up. I chose to learn from my mistakes and keep moving forward. I hope this will be true for you as well.

YOUR TURN

Think about someone you know who has been successful. Can you discern whether they have a fixed or a growth mindset? Notice how they confront hard issues and obstacles. Are there things they do to stretch themselves, even if they know they might fail?

Make a list of two or three people you admire and trust for their positive contributions to your life or to your community. Contact them and ask them if they have some time to sit down and talk with you about their path in life. Asking questions and learning from others is one of the best ways to grow, and most successful people are happy to share their stories with individuals who are curious and ask good questions.

People to contact:

_____

_____

_____

_____

_____

_____

_____

DIG DEEPER

READ

- *Mindset: The New Psychology of Success* by Carol Dweck
- *Gmorning, Gnight!: Little Pep Talks for Me & You* by Lin-Manuel Miranda and Jonny Sun
- *How Full is Your Bucket?* by Tom Rath and Donald O. Clifton, PhD.
- *The Storyteller's Secret: From TED Speakers to Business Legends, Why Some Ideas Catch On and Others Don't* by Carmine Gallo

LISTEN

- *Impact Theory* podcast with Tom Bilyeu
- *The Mindset Mentor* podcast with Rob Dial
- *Little Inner Voice* podcast
- *Oprah's SuperSoul Conversations:* Oprah and Joel Osteen—I am: Life is How You See It

WATCH

- *Grit: the power of passion and perseverance* | Angela *Lee Duckworth—TED Talk*
- *The Secret of Becoming Mentally Strong* | Amy Morin—TEDxOcala

---

ACTION STEPS

List some of the negative self-talk that you've experienced (fixed mindset). What does it say? When is it the loudest?

Now list some of the positive self-talk (growth mindset) that you have used. How do you react when you decide to face your day with a positive rather than a negative viewpoint?

What happens when your negative voice wins?

What happens when your positive voice wins?

Which voice wins most often?

What are three or four specific steps you can take to increase your acceptance of your most positive inclinations and attitudes?

What internal reminders can you use to notice the negative voice and then "reframe" your thoughts when things aren't going well?

The most powerful weapon on earth is
the human soul on fire.

—FRENCH WWI FIELD MARSHALL FERDINAND FOCH

CHAPTER 2

FIND AND FOLLOW A PASSION

When I was in college, I started a driveway blacktop sealing business. It was hot, sweaty work during Cincinnati summers, but I loved the flexibility of creating a business on my own terms and not having a cap on the money I could earn or the opportunities for growth I could consider.

As I watched my buddies work summer jobs they hated at minimum wage, I knew I wanted something different. I also noticed I was drawn to the idea of creating a business out of nothing to see if I could grow it into something bigger—all while earning the money I needed to help pay for college.

During this time, an important seed was planted: a growing passion around the idea of becoming an entrepreneur. I could see myself starting and growing a business one day, and that excited me.

The opportunity to spend our lives doing work we love is something most of us dream about. When we envision our future, it involves a life and career built around doing something that energizes us and makes us excited to get up in the morning and get moving. That's why finding something we can be passionate about is so crucial. It can fuel our vision for the future and help guide our decisions—both small and large—along the way.

PURSUING A PAYCHECK

Many college graduates take their first job with no real sense for what they want to "be" when they grow up. Friends and family give them advice. They make use of their network and search online for opportunities. They start interviewing for jobs that might be a fit. Many times, facing the bills that come as they move out on their own, they interview simply to secure their first real paycheck.

They move into adult life hoping it all works out, but not really knowing how to approach the small and large choices that will eventually move them toward (or away from) their dreams. They hope somehow everything they've learned in school will apply to real life. They hope they'll find happiness along the way. But hope is not a strategy.

When they start going to work and receiving that coveted paycheck, everything seems good—*until* they realize that while the money might be decent, the work certainly is not.

So they leave their first job for another one. And then another. They bounce around, trying new things, gaining new experience, and potentially making more money, but never really enjoying the work. It can all end up feeling like a never-ending cycle. Soon, they settle for less than they've always dreamed about and begin simply working for the weekend—or anticipating their two weeks of vacation—rather than living in full pursuit of their passions and interests.

But it doesn't have to be this way.

My hope is that this chapter will serve as a starting point in directing you toward a passion that can fuel a very different vision for your future.

PINPOINTING A PASSION

You might already recognize a few of the things you're passionate about—a skill or talent comes easily to you or something energizes or excites you. For example, if you love numbers, maybe you imagine yourself as a CPA or a commercial banker at a great firm. If you're energized by competition, perhaps you hope to become a successful salesperson, business owner or entrepreneur. If you're creative, you might see yourself as an architect, graphic designer, Illustrator or musician. If you're service minded, you might be interested in being a teacher, therapist or nurse.

But what if you're not sure what you're passionate about? That's OK too! It's easy to get stuck right here, feeling like you can't move forward until you've identified that one thing that's going to fuel you and drive you toward your future.

Instead of focusing on what you don't know, think about what you do know. Pay attention to the things that energize you. Notice how you feel about each aspect of your current job—the things you enjoy doing and what you'd love to never have to do again.

If you're still in school, think about the courses you're taking. Are there specific tasks or projects that you most enjoy? Are there subjects you gravitate toward? Are there areas in your life where you feel you're making a difference or finding success? Move toward those.

It might also be helpful to consider what you already do just because you enjoy it. Are you consistently directing your time, money and energy toward certain things? For example, does beating your personal best when running give you an adrenaline boost? Are you energized by juggling all the details involved in organizing for a cause or event you care about? Do you feel excitement (or even a bit of fear) when you imagine a specific possibility for your future? These are all important clues for finding things that drive you.

Finally, talk to others about what they see in you—what they envision you doing for a living or where they see you gaining energy. It's always helpful to get an outside perspective from those who know you best so you can explore possibilities that would never have occurred to you otherwise.

PICKING A PATH

Once you've gathered your information and ideas, pick a path that interests and energizes you most. Don't let yourself become paralyzed by all the possibilities. The important thing is to simply get started. Choose something you feel you can be passionate about at this moment in your life, set your sights on the first step or two, and go for it. See where those first steps lead you. If you discover later that you want to take a different path altogether, it's okay. Experience helps you find your way forward. The important thing is to take action and get started:

1. Begin with a first step

Clarity starts with *taking* action, not just *thinking* about it. (Reread the quote by Roosevelt in the opening pages of this book for additional inspiration.) By picking a place to get started and taking your first steps forward, you can begin to get experience that will help inform your vision for the future.

Maybe that first step begins with a bit of research. Maybe it starts with a conversation. Perhaps it leads you to apply for a specific internship or job opportunity. Whatever it is, as long as it's a step forward, you're making progress.

A great example of this comes in training for a 5K. You have to first lace your shoes and either get on a treadmill or go outside. Walking becomes jogging and jogging becomes running. And before you know it, you're crossing the finish line. Finding a passion begins with taking that critical first step.

2. Success brings opportunity

Being good at something creates more opportunities for you. If you work hard to be successful in the work you do each day, additional opportunities will likely come your way. A manager who sees an employee working diligently and enjoying their job tends to give that employee more chances to learn and grow. A positive attitude can get you selected for a project that could lead toward personal and professional growth. Making a commitment to do solid work each day will often pay real-time dividends.

As you learn more about your interests, use this time to read widely (see the list of resources at the end of this chapter to get you started) and seek out training opportunities through your job or other online courses related to your interests. It might be helpful to ask others in your organization about training opportunities available to you—both in-house and outside. Do your research, then make a list of the potential benefits to the company if you acquire these skills and approach your supervisor with the request. An employee who is proactively sharpening their skills is a valuable asset to any organization.

There are also many books and online resources focused on helping you discover your strengths, and quite often these tools are available to employees through their human resources department, so this is a great place to start. Resources like this will help you discover more about yourself so you can continue to develop personally and professionally. Life is a continual learning process for all of us, and taking time to learn new things can often lead toward uncovering interests and passions we've not considered before.

3. Opportunity can lead to finding a passion

By taking advantage of growth opportunities that are presented, you can begin to get a sense of what you enjoy and where your most productive interests lie. Make the most of these opportunities and let them inform and guide you. Follow your curiosity toward the things that give you the most energy.

Don't worry about getting everything exactly right. The point is to start somewhere and begin the process of learning more about yourself. No matter what, you'll become a more well-rounded person and a more valuable asset to any organization.

4. Leave room for growth and change

A key aspect to remember in your search for a passion is that it is not static. What you're passionate about will likely grow and change with you in life. You might be passionate about something in this season of your life and then find that it morphs into another one a few years later. This is an important concept to understand so that we don't lock ourselves into thinking we can only have one passion the rest of our lives. It also takes some pressure off those who think they have to hurry up and find a passion. Passions will grow and change with us; expect that to be true and allow for it.

START WITH STEPPING-STONES

Following your passion doesn't necessarily mean you'll immediately find your dream job and only do work you love from day one. You will likely start in an entry-level position that will include aspects you don't enjoy . . . and that's completely normal. The important thing is to feel like your work is preparing and developing you to one day reach your dreams. If you can see your early experience as a stepping-stone to eventually getting where you want to be, then it's an important part of your journey.

For example, inputting sales forecasting numbers into a spreadsheet may not be the most exciting thing you've ever done, but it does give you an insider view of the company's short- and long-term goals. If you begin to understand those figures, you'll gain more insights that will be valuable to your supervisors.

Maybe assembling PowerPoint presentations for your team makes your eyes cross, but if you innovate and use your creative energy to make them more efficient and interesting, you can distinguish yourself as a clear communicator with great ideas for the organization. In these ways, you can begin to make intentional, positive steps toward learning more about your interests and further defining your goals for tomorrow.

FUEL YOUR FUTURE

In our next chapter, we'll talk about creating your life vision—dreaming big, writing those dreams down and sharing them. Vision is what sets the table for the rest of your life. The specificity of your vision may change and morph slightly over time, along with your passions, but it does help you get started on a definitive path. Your life vision, fueled by passion, will serve as the compass to direct your decisions. That vision can help you see how taking (or even turning down) a specific job might be the right stepping-stone for you. It can keep you focused on your future and allow you to filter decisions based on where you want to be someday. It can give you the courage to remain focused on your passions, not on your fears.

This is why finding and following a passion is so important: it will help you stay focused on doing the kind of work that truly energizes you, and it will help fuel your vision for the future. And, as I have learned from my own experience, it will literally change the course of your life.

MY STORY

My first job out of college at Procter & Gamble involved calling on grocery stores to sell laundry and dishwashing detergent to store managers. Truthfully, I was not passionate about selling soap. But I *was* passionate about my dream to one day start, grow and run a business.

I knew this work experience would provide great sales training for my future benefit, and that it could give me the opportunity to move into management at a relatively young age. All this was helping to prepare me for my ultimate goal of starting my own business one day. Because of this, I viewed my first job as a stepping-stone toward my dream. Having a clear vision for the long term helped push me forward and keep me from getting stuck, even when I didn't really enjoy the work.

Your first job may not be your dream job. But if you stay focused on your dreams and pay attention to your passions, the experiences you gain in your early career can help prepare you and lead you to where you want to go.

A quote that is attributed to many great thinkers says, "Find a job doing something you love and you'll never have to work a day in your life." Pursuing something you love allows you to pour your heart into everything you do. For me, it has also served as the fuel to keep going during tough times. As you saw in chapter 1 and will read in many of the following pages, it has also helped me overcome obstacles that otherwise might have stopped me in my tracks. Without passion, I would never have been inspired to think bigger and go after my dreams, even during hard times.

Today, I can say that I walk into my office every day excited about my work. I love what I do and the people I work with—and that is one of the most amazing feelings in the world.

My passion for building something from nothing and the goal of starting my own business were seeds that grew into my vision and plans for the future—and they gave me the tenacity I needed to never give up on my dreams.

YOUR TURN

What do you feel passionate about? If you're not sure, consider what you're curious about. Think about your natural talents, hobbies and interests. Perhaps, start by remembering what you loved doing as a kid. Finally, ask others who know you well if there are things they've noticed you're especially good at.

Notice when you enjoy doing something. Jot down some notes as you do these things to see if you can find a few common themes. Then find someone you trust to help you process what you've learned so far. An outside perspective can be extremely helpful when you're trying to find clarity on an issue as personal as this one.

Don't be afraid to call someone with a career you find interesting and ask them how they got started. You will likely find that most people who love what they do also love to talk with others about it!

Finally, remember that people don't just have one passion; there are many areas that we can become passionate about. By trying new things and taking on new opportunities, we can find new interests and passions that we enjoy and want to work toward.

DIG DEEPER

READ

- *Strengths Finder 2.0* by Tom Rath
- *Designing Your Life: How to Build a Well-Lived, Joyful Life* by Bill Burnett and Dave Evans
- *What Color Is Your Parachute?* by Richard Nelson Bolles
- *Think and Grow Rich* by Napoleon Hill
- *Are you Fully Charged?* by Tom Rath
- *Start with Why: How Great Leaders Inspire Everyone to Take Action* by Simon Sinek
- *The Road Back to You* by Ian Cron and Susan Stabile

LISTEN

- *Oprah's SuperSoul Conversations:* Elizabeth Gilbert: *The Curiousity-Driven Life*
- *Motiv8 — The Motivation and Inspiration Podcast*
- *The TED Interview* podcast. Head of TED, Chris Andersen, speaks with some of the world's most interesting people to dig into the provocative and powerful ideas of our time.
- *The Motivated Mind* Episode 4: Your Passion—Focus on it
- *The Good Life Project* podcast by Jonathon Fields; take the Sparketype assessment at *goodlifeproject.com/sparketest*

WATCH

- *2 questions to uncover your passion—and turn it into a career* | Noeline Kirabo—TED Talk
- *Find your dream job without ever looking at your resume* | Laura Berman Fortgang—TED Talk

- -

ACTION STEPS

Once you make the list of your talents and passions, make a list of the types of jobs, careers or industries that might be interesting to you. Think about who in your family or professional network has access to information that would be helpful to you, and then take the first step toward learning more about the ones that most interest you.

Talents and Passions:

Careers and industries of interest:

Never give up on what you really want to do.
The person with big dreams is more powerful
than one with all the facts.

—ALBERT EINSTEIN

Create the highest, grandest vision possible for your life,
because you become what you believe.

—OPRAH WINFREY

Stick your neck out. . . . It's a lot more fun than sitting
at home watching other people do It.

—SIR RICHARD BRANSON

CHAPTER 3

DREAM BIG . . .
THEN MAKE IT BIGGER!

A critical next step toward achieving your dreams is envisioning the kind of future you want.

For me, I knew in high school after I started a lawn mowing business with my brothers that I wanted to be an entrepreneur. I pictured myself starting and growing a successful business. I loved the idea of eventually selling that business for a strong return and then starting a new venture. I often imagined the excitement I'd feel when I reached that goal. In addition, I saw myself happily married with a family and involved in my community.

At first, this vision bounced around in my head. Over time, I learned from others about the importance of actually writing a vision down to help crystallize my dreams and clarify my thoughts. Although I was introduced to this idea of writing my vision down when I was in my twenties, I didn't really understand the power of it until I was in my thirties and began to see how having a tangible reminder made a difference (to this day I keep my vision statement in my briefcase).

Thinking big, actually writing goals down and then revisiting them regularly has worked well for me and for others I know. So well, in fact, that I now encourage everyone I know to do the same.

GETTING CLARITY

Your greatest hopes and dreams are likely already inside your head, and you've known about them for a while.

Maybe you've spent a lot of time thinking about them and strategizing how to make those dreams a reality. You've likely added to them while driving, during school or work or perhaps you wake up thinking about your future goals.

You might also question yourself sometimes, wondering if your dreams are realistic or if they could ever really come true. Are they too big? Can you generate the resources to make them a reality?

Perhaps you've dismissed them because you're afraid that you don't have what it takes. You might even feel like your hopes and dreams are still unclear—as if they're a tiny seed of an idea waiting to be watered so they can grow when the time is right.

Regardless of where you are right now you have the opportunity to completely change your life—if you take the time to start envisioning the kind of future you want. As you begin to define and clarify them, these dreams will begin to play a key role in providing direction and answers for your future.

CREATING YOUR VISION

Time Is almost always the enemy of pursuing our dreams. If we allow our dreams to kick around in our head, year after year, but we don't move toward making them a reality, our dreams will begin to dissipate and feel far away. If left unattended, we will eventually come to see them as just "wishful thinking" and begin to regret not taking action.

I've met so many people in their fifties and sixties who express regret over never pursuing their dreams. Because they were unable to transfer their dreams into a clear vision and specific goals, they never took action and nothing happened. Today, they regretfully talk about "what might have been" had they taken action when they were younger.

How can you begin to define your dreams now and create a clear vision for your future?

First, invest the time to create a specific picture of who you want to become, what you want to accomplish and how you will feel living this future life. Be future-focused, and as you think about these things, remember to be as specific as possible. Find a quiet, peaceful place as you consider this, and ask yourself:

What would my extraordinary life feel like?

Start by eliminating all constraints and allowing yourself to think big. Go deeper by answering some of these questions about your life in this future state:

- What kinds of things am I doing each day that I love to do? What am I doing both professionally and personally that energizes me?

- What accomplishments and successes have I achieved that I'm most proud of?
- What kind of person am I? What are my values? How are my family relationships?
- Where would I live? What's the first thing I do when I wake up? How would I dress? What does my daily schedule look like?
- Who is around me? Who are the people most inspiring to me? Would any of these people be working with me to fulfill my dreams? How do others describe me?

Write down everything that comes to mind in as much detail as possible. Start with bullets, then add more specifics to paint the most vivid picture possible.

Then look at it again. Is it extraordinary? Are you pleased with this picture? If not, rewrite it, and consider making it bigger. Your vision will pull you to your future if you stay focused on it. So, think about it in a big way, not in a modest way. Let possibility and "what if" thinking guide you as you write it down. The most important element in all of this is that your vision grabs your imagination.

Ask yourself three questions:

1. Does it *excite* me?
2. Do I feel *energized* when I think about it?
3. Do I know why I want to achieve it so badly?

This passion around your "why" will drive you and provide the "juice" to keep you moving forward, even when things get tough. It will drive your personal commitment and will be the reason you're willing to do the hard work to make your dreams come true. It will provide the motivation you need to get up when you fall down. And, it will help you to be bold as you move forward, step-by-step, no matter what life throws your way.

Remember this: you are the only one who can hold yourself back from creating the kind of life you imagine.

The things that have happened to this point in your life don't define you, even if they have been incredibly difficult. Negative things others have said about you don't have to define you unless you choose to let them. Break free from doubt. Your future begins today. As you follow the next steps, take your time and describe everything in as much detail as you can, envisioning your life as if you've already achieved it.

As you create your vision and goals, five things are critically important:

1. Write your vision down

As you begin to see your dreams, capture that picture in your mind and make it as vivid as possible. Physically write down what you've conceived while answering the questions above. You can use the outline I've provided at the end of this chapter as a starting point.

Don't worry yet about all the details of *how* you'll make everything happen. Your list doesn't have to be perfect—you can always make tweaks along the way and return to it again and again as you find more inspiration or information. This is a working document.

Putting pen to paper can turn a fleeting dream into a powerful vision. When you physically write your vision down, it gets etched in your mind. As you review it, your mind subconsciously opens itself up to possibility and begins to help you work toward your goals.

This one simple action will dramatically increase the chances of your dreams coming true. You'll also find that writing down your vision statement solidifies It in your subconscious mind, becoming a powerful tool to direct your future decisions.

2. Then make it bigger!

When I first began to dream about being an entrepreneur, I simply knew I wanted to start a company and make it successful. I wasn't sure exactly what that meant or what it would look like. But as the years went by and I was ready to start Fusion Education Group (the company I now run), I knew I wanted it to grow well beyond one or two schools.

Who are the key people in your life with whom you share your dreams? If there aren't any, jot down a few names of people you'd like to get to know better.

I wanted Fusion to become a leading provider of personalized education and someday grow to over a hundred schools across the country. But in order to make that big idea happen, I needed to raise a lot of money from investors. I wasn't just looking at the challenge of raising a few dollars to get started—I needed $40 million.

Many people thought I was crazy, and a lot of investors turned me down (see chapter 5 for the story of how I raised these funds), but I knew significant capital would be needed to grow a healthy company of that size. If I skimped, we'd always be short on funds.

At the time I wrote down my vision to someday get to one hundred schools, we had very little chance of making it a reality. In fact, many visitors to our first tiny office laughed when they saw the big vision statement displayed on a giant piece of foam core behind the front desk in our entryway. But what I've learned over time is that if you write your dreams down and then revisit them to make them even bigger, well beyond your current realm of possibility, you'll be surprised at what you will accomplish. As you create your big-dream goals and discuss them with others, the very repetition of the conversations you have will naturally help you internalize your future success and move you toward the actions to make these happen.

Today Fusion is almost to its big-dream goal of one hundred schools. This concept of making my dreams even bigger forced me to think much more strategically, recruit more talented partners and plan future actions that would allow this kind of goal to eventually become a reality.

Big successes don't just happen. Each one starts with thinking big, setting goals, writing them down and raising the bar of our own expectations and the expectations of others. It creates a common objective for the future. Thinking differently is the key to making big dreams happen.

3. Share your vision with those you trust

We all need people in our lives who also dream big and are pursuing their own challenging goals. If your world is largely full of friends, siblings and colleagues who tell you your dreams are unimportant, too big to achieve, or simply not worth it, then you need to think about adding a few new people into your life.

Find people to associate with who will push you to new heights. Spend time with friends who won't let you simply give up when you face obstacles or setbacks. When you find friends who believe in you, you can trust them with your dreams because you know they won't dismiss or belittle them.

If you don't already have similar people like this in your life, start thinking about how you might find a few. Who do you admire and trust, even from afar? Who do you know that is looking for more with their life? Who shows high levels of drive and commitment? Be proactive and reach out to them. Invite them to coffee or to lunch to discuss how they pursued (or are pursuing) their own path. If they're open to the possibility, you might consider asking them to become a mentor or an accountability partner. Successful people are typically willing to help others succeed as a way of giving back.

4. Put your vision where you see it every day

Once the first draft of your vision is solidified, put what you have written in a place where you can see it every day. I typed mine up, laminated it and posted it in my bathroom. To this day, I keep it in my briefcase so it's with me wherever I go.

But you might choose to go another route and make a more creative display you can frame, like a vision board or a PowerPoint presentation that you can view on your laptop or phone each day. Choose an option that works best for you to keep your dreams front and center in your life and to encourage you each day, and especially during challenging times.

5. Revisit your vision and goals regularly

Take the time to formally revisit your vision statement each year. Are there tweaks you want to make or things you'd like to change? Pull out your three- to five-year goals and review your one-year goals. (If you don't have those yet, don't worry. There's a framework at the end of this chapter to help you.) Is what you're doing today building toward the long-term vision you want to achieve? At the end of each quarter (every three months), set action plans to move you toward your goals during the ensuing ninety days. This regular review and short term goal setting is the key to achieving a big vision and long-term goals— breaking them down into manageable chunks and working on small steps every week or month.

Also, sometimes doors to our dreams close and we have to reevaluate. This means taking a step back to revisit our vision. Does it need to change completely? Or can you still reach your goal by taking a different path?

These are all important questions to ask on a regular basis. It takes a lot of grit to face a setback, reevaluate, develop a new strategy, and then keep going. But that's also the beauty of being human. We can learn, and we can adapt and take comfort in the fact that there is never just one route to happiness, to success or to a vision.

MY STORY

Dreaming Big: Part 1

During college, I had a semester long internship in Dallas, Texas, with a business owner named David Morehead. One day, as we were driving to a meeting, David asked me about my goals and we discussed them for a while. That's when he asked me if I had ever considered going to business school.

No one in my family had ever gone to business school, and while I had certainly thought about it, I never seriously considered it as a real possibility. I wasn't confident I could even get into a top school, so I answered David's question with a simple, "No, I haven't."

In the course of our conversation that day, David encouraged me to not only consider business school, but to make getting into Harvard Business School my goal. Harvard obviously wasn't even on my radar at that time. On that day, it seemed like a huge, out-of-reach goal. But somehow David convinced me I had the ability to do it.

His belief in me changed my mindset and fueled my vision to dream big and go for it. If it hadn't been for David planting that seed, I would never have considered Harvard. As I look back today, I can say that one conversation single-handedly raised my own expectations for myself and my future. That's the power of even a small amount of encouragement from someone you trust.

This is why surrounding yourself with others who dream big is so important—when others believe in you and encourage you to pursue what might seem like a wild dream, you start to think maybe you *can* achieve those goals. As you begin to envision them, you slowly start to believe in the possibility. Once you let your mind start to see your limitless potential, it's amazing what can happen.

After that conversation in the car, I wrote down my big-dream goal: to attend Harvard. It changed how I approached the rest of my college experience and influenced the positions I took as my first job after school. I upgraded my own expectations and started making decisions that would help increase my chances of getting into the program on which I had set my sights. Eventually, because of that one conversation, that one seed planted, and that person who believed in me, I was able to make it happen.

Dreaming Big: Part 2

Fast-forward twenty years, and the power of writing down my dreams continued to play a big role in my life. When I first wrote out my vision to go to business school, it was simple and without a lot of detail. But as I grew older, I began to notice the power of recording and revisiting these goals, and so I put more time and effort into the process, which meant writing them out in more and more detail. I also began to formally revisit my lifetime vision statement annually to refine and update it.

By the time I was in my forties, I was really struggling with a career decision I'd made and the fact that I'd taken a position that ended up being completely wrong for me. I was down on myself, frustrated and knew I needed to figure out what to do and where to go next.

After some soul-searching, I decided to rewrite my vision statement from scratch. This time I put more details in it. It wasn't limited to just my career, but it also included my vision for my family, my values and my personal life. Revisioning my future during this dark time ended up giving me the boost I needed to stop feeling sorry for myself, to clarify what mattered most to me and to become proactive in defining the future I wanted. It not only solidified that I was not in the job role I wanted, but it also gave me much needed energy and passion for making my next move. Creating this clear vision gave me the courage I needed to make the tough call to leave this role, start new and pursue a career I really wanted.

Writing your vision down in detail can help to define and solidify your destination in your mind. The more descriptive you are and the more details you include, the better chance you have to create a picture you believe in and the clarity you need to begin taking action. Later in this chapter, I've included the actual vision statement I created during the dark time I mentioned above as an example and a bit of inspiration for creating your own.

YOUR TURN

CREATING AND BUILDING A PLAN TO ACHIEVE YOUR BIG-VISION EXERCISE

Now is the time to take all that you've learned in this chapter and all the notes you've jotted down and use them to create your first official big-dream vision statement.

Describe how you see your life ten to twenty-five years from now. Make it as detailed as possible, as if you're writing a news article about your life at that time. Write about your professional career, your family, your personal life, your hobbies, your health, your finances, your spiritual health, your values and what you stand for. Note how you spend your time, where you live, what you enjoy doing. The more descriptive you can make it, the better.

Next, write out your goals for the next three to five years. Taking the time to do this can make your long-term vision seem much more manageable and ensure that what you're working on today are stepping-stones to where you'd like to be in the future.

When creating these goals, ask, "What things do I want to accomplish over this time frame?" Your goals should be focused on major achievements you're targeting, new or improved skills, expertise or experiences you'll need to build. These are the major milestones designed to best position you to achieve your long-term vision. To help organize your thoughts, think of them in terms of categories:

a. Professional Goals
b. Personal Health Goals
c. Spiritual Goals
d. Financial Goals
e. Family Goals

Later, we'll work on creating annual and quarterly priorities necessary to move toward achieving these three-to-five year objectives.

Below is the vision statement I created for myself back in 2005. Feel free to use it as an example to help you get started. Or use your own creativity to create a vision that inspires you. You may even want to take this vision statement and create a visual representation, or vision board, of your limitless future.

PETER G. RUPPERT
Personal Vision Statement
November, 2005
As I look to the future, every day will be bright and full of opportunity. I will wake up each day with a zest for life and full of energy to do great things. I will honor God and strive to do his will on this earth. I will make my family my top priority and have a strong, loving, and ever-improving relationship with my wife. I will be an outstanding father and invest in creating great one-on-one relationships with each of my children. I will be there to support, encourage, and discipline them while ensuring that they learn to deal with disappointment,

understand the value of hard work and dedication, and passionately pursue their own dreams.

By the time I am 43, I will have started my own company where I will create a national, industry-leading organization that attracts talented people committed to our company vision and who are empowered to achieve their potential through significant responsibility, authority, and accountability in their individual roles. Ideally, the company I start will be in an industry focused on helping people improve their lives. By the time I am 53, I will have created a personal net worth of $_____ and will earn $_____ annually.

I will maintain a balanced life at all times and will strive to continually stretch myself and learn new things. I will continue to enhance my leadership skills and my speaking skills so that someday I can get paid for my public speaking. I will strive to be a leader who attracts other leaders and who reaches out to and mentors young people. Finally, I will give back in both financial and personal ways to help the young and the struggling.

When life is complete, people will remember me for having a great marriage, for raising great kids who are successfully pursuing their dreams, and for a successful career that had a positive impact on the lives of many and was a changing force for the better in America.

MY BIG VISION (10-25 YEARS FROM NOW)

Clearly lay out details of your extraordinary life 10-25 years from now. Think of a news article describing your life at that time. Write about your professional career, your family, your health, your finances, your faith, your values, etc.

_____

_____

_____

_____

_____

_____

_____

MY 3-5 YEAR GOALS/MILESTONES

List major achievements you are targeting, new or improved skills, expertise, or experiences you'll need to build.

Professional Goals

Personal/Health Goals

Family/Relationships Goals

Financial Goals

Spiritual Goals

DIG DEEPER

READ

- *The Art of Dreaming Big* by Lu Anne Puett
- *Trillion Dollar Coach: The Leadership Playbook of Silicon Valley's Bill Campbell* by Alan Eagle, Eric Schmidt and Jonathan Rosenberg
- *Life in Motion: An Unlikely Ballerina* by Misty Copeland and Charisse Jones
- *The Vision Board: The Secret to an Extraordinary Life* by Joyce Schwarz

LISTEN

- *TED Radio Hour* podcast
- *How I Built This* podcast, hosted by Guy Raz
- *Dream Big* podcast with Bob Goff
- *The Learning Leader* podcast with Ryan Hawk

WATCH

- *The Power of Vision* by Joel Barker—Discovering the Future Series by Media Partners
- *The Secret* by TS Production, LLC
- *Jim Carrey's 2014 commencement address* at Maharishi University of Management
- *How to DREAM Big and achieve your goals and dreams.* | Ian Hacon—TEDxNorwichED
- *How to Create a Vision Board video* by Jack Canfield. https://youtu.be/iamZEW0x3dM

ACTION STEPS

SHOW AND TELL

Now that you have your vision and goals written out, it's time to take some action!

First, find at least one or two people with whom you can share your new vision statement and the shorter-term goals to get you there. Ask them questions to probe whether they have ideas for an even larger vision you can aspire to.

Next, go back and revise your vision based on what you've learned. Did you discover ways you could make it even bigger? In what ways might you stretch yourself even further than you'd imagined as you write out this second draft?

Finally, find a visible place to keep your vision so that you can readily see it and read it every day. Make a plan to formally revisit your vision statement and goals regularly (typically every year for your vision and every ninety days for your goals) and mark the dates on your calendar so you can ensure you'll make it happen!

Review your long-term vision statement again.
Is it big enough? If not, revisit and make it bigger.

Who can you share your new vision with?

Where can you post it so you see and read it every day?

*A mentor is someone who allows you to see
the hope inside yourself.*

—OPRAH WINFREY

*Keep away from those who try to belittle your
ambitions. Small people always do that. But the really
great make you believe that you, too, can become great.*

—MARK TWAIN

*If I have seen further it is by standing on
the shoulders of giants.*

—SIR ISAAC NEWTON

*A mentor is someone who sees more talent
and ability within you, than you see in yourself,
and helps bring it out of you.*

—BOB PROCTOR

*Show me a successful individual and I'll show you
someone who had real, positive influences in his or her
life. I don't care what you do for a living—if you do it
well I'm sure there was someone cheering you
on or showing the way. A mentor.*

—DENZEL WASHINGTON

CHAPTER 4

FIND A CHAMPION

WE ALL NEED CHAMPIONS

Before the underdog North Carolina State men's basketball team made its legendary 6-0 run to win the 1983 NCAA Championship, coach Jimmy Valvano's dad already had his suitcase packed and ready to go. It turns out he'd had his suitcase packed for years, waiting for the day he'd get to travel to watch his son's team win a national title.

Well before Jimmy ever got to coach at a big-time program like NC State, he had repeatedly told his dad about his dream. He had long before established his own big vision to win the NCAA national championship someday. A few days after Jimmy—a young, newly-hired head coach at a tiny school—first told his dad about that dream, his dad showed him his packed suitcase and said, "Son, my bags are already packed."

Year after year, as Jimmy progressed in his career, they would have the same exchange. Later, after achieving his lifelong dream, Jimmy would often say, "My father gave me the greatest gift anyone could give another person . . . he believed in me."

Everyone needs a champion like this in his or her life. A champion is a huge supporter, a person you can confide in. You can talk to them about your dreams, frustrations and challenges, and then expect honest, supportive feedback. Mentors like these have provided valuable perspective and feedback throughout my own life and for many of my friends as well.

Spending time with a champion who has been down a similar path as the one you want to walk and who has experienced his/her own successes and failures along the way can shorten your learning curve and encourage you to move forward in the right direction. Champions serve three crucial roles in our life and the lives of those around us:

1. Sounding board

We all need a safe and supportive environment to share our ideas and dreams. A mentor provides a sounding board to encourage and even challenge us at times, all with an aim of refining our perspectives and goals. Having someone to listen to our vision and respond with wisdom and support is of enormous practical benefit. Make it a goal to find someone who is willing to discuss your long and short term goals and provide support and feedback along your journey. Also, ask them to advise you about potential pitfalls you might experience along the way.

2. Support

A champion provides the support you need to keep dreaming big. They sometimes see things you haven't yet seen in yourself. They believe in you, can encourage you in your pursuits and they're willing to help you to get where you want to go.

3. Accountability

When times get tough, a champion is there to encourage you to keep going. They can hold you accountable to your goals and help you get back up after you fail. They don't let you feel sorry for yourself. They restore your faith in yourself and help you reclaim your motivation to keep moving forward. Or, when needed, they can help you regroup and approach your goals from a different direction or perspective.

TALK ABOUT IT

When it comes to making your dreams come true, there are two foundational steps that are absolutely required. We already talked about the first step: getting clear on your vision and writing it down in as much detail as possible so you can start to internalize it, sear it in your mind and work toward accomplishing it.

The second part of making your dreams a reality is talking about them. The act of verbalizing them to someone else is another step toward commitment. As you talk about your vision for the future, you will clarify

Do you have any champions in your life today? If so, who? What role(s) do they play?

and refine it. As you spend time in conversation, you begin to imagine your goals in even more detail. By doing this, you will actually be training your brain to subconsciously help you find a way to meet your goals.

The more you talk about your vision with others, the more likely you are to eventually achieve it. Verbalizing it with someone makes it all the more real and helps spark the motivation you need to keep working toward your goals. It encourages you to take action because once you've shared it with others, it's harder for you to talk yourself out of it. You're committed and your champion is now aware and there to help!

A personal example is my long-time friendship with David Morehead, the mentor I first mentioned in chapter 3. As I look back, I can see the important influence he has been in my life. During my internship, he took the time to give me projects that helped me learn more about business. We had numerous conversations about goals and dreams. He even occasionally invited me to his house to have dinner with his family. When he encouraged me to pursue business school, it literally changed my life and how I approached my next few years.

Throughout my entrepreneurial journey, I have periodically kept in touch with David. We would occasionally exchange emails and phone calls. Every year, we have shared Christmas cards. On my way to vacation in New Mexico one year, my family and I met him and his wife for lunch in Santa Fe, where he got to meet my kids for the first time. When we sold our company a while back, I reached out and sent him the press release.

I know David appreciated the fact that I kept in touch throughout the years, and though our conversations have been intermittent over time, they've been important in my life as I've continued to solidify and reach for my dreams. I have so much respect for all he did for me during those early years when I was trying to determine what I wanted to do and who I wanted to be. That single conversation about business school and his insight into my abilities literally changed the trajectory of my life.

This exemplifies why I encourage everyone to seek out others who are better, smarter and more successful (so far) in their own work and in life. They are the people who can inspire you through their own example. None of us can do everything on our own; no matter how smart we are, we still need the benefit of the perspectives and feedback of others. Indeed, the more champions we have in our lives, the better.

FINDING YOUR CHAMPIONS

Many people ask me about the best way to find a mentor, and my answer is always simple: "Just ask."

In life, we get what we ask for and what we are willing to act on. So, don't allow yourself to sit on the sidelines wishing you had a mentor or believing it's too hard to find one.

Simply make the effort to find one, then ask if they would be willing to give you some of their time and attention.

You'll find that most successful people realize they're standing on the shoulders of those who helped **them** find success, and they usually want to pay it forward. But even if the person you approach says no, why not use it as an opportunity to ask them to recommend someone else in your field of interest?

Sometimes it may take time to find a mentor who's walked ahead of you in terms of age and success, so if you haven't found that person yet, look for a peer or colleague who also isn't comfortable with simply maintaining the status quo in their own life. Find someone your age who is also pursuing great things . . . someone who has a similar mindset and who is committed to their own growth and development. As you meet to discuss your plans, you can then help each other in the pursuit of your

Is there someone you think might make a good mentor? Start making a list today of possible people to contact.

respective dreams, even if they're dramatically different. All you need is a friendly and supportive sounding board to talk with about your dreams.

Trying to pursue your vision by yourself is hard, so find a champion (or champions) who can help you get there by being there along the way.

MY STORY

Some of the most important champions in my life have been a small group of like-minded peers.

In my mid-thirties I joined an organization called Young Presidents Organization (YPO). Within YPO, individuals then join small groups of seven to nine executives in mini organizations called forums. I joined YPO and my forum group for an opportunity to network and build relationships with others who had similar goals and desires to improve professionally and personally.

Throughout the years, our forum group has met every few months for a half-day ending with dinner together. Once a year we also attend a retreat and spend time in deep conversations reviewing our goals and discussing opportunities and challenges in our business and personal lives.

This tight knit group has provided me the opportunity for deep, trusting friendships and a vehicle to have open, honest conversations on important topics. Over time, we have become comfortable sharing our problems, concerns, issues and feelings with one another. Whether we're facing challenges related to personal, family or business matters, we know we're in a safe and trusting environment of mutual support and camaraderie.

During a particularly challenging time in my own life when I was unemployed, I was nervously considering trying to raise money to pursue my dream of starting a company, rather than doing the easier and more expected thing: simply focusing on finding another job. The encouragement and support I received from this group were vital in helping me find the courage to pursue starting a business. If they hadn't believed in me and firmly encouraged my efforts, making the ultimate decision to follow my dream and start my company would have been much harder.

One person in my forum group, Mark Bissell, offered some great wisdom I will never forget. Early on in my decision process, I was deliberating over several potential new business opportunities that spanned a few different industries, but Mark sensed what I really should do was to get back into education. He asked why I would consider walking away from all the success and expertise I'd built up over the years as an executive in the education industry to start a new business in a different industry.

I needed to hear that exact message at the time because I still wasn't confident enough to believe I could pull off a new startup in the education industry. Mark's encouraging advice was what I needed to help me realize I did have the track record, skills and experience to make the commitment and move forward. He helped me narrow my focus, realize what I wanted, and reinforced the importance of believing in myself.

Trying to accomplish our goals and dreams without support from others is extremely challenging. It can be lonely, and if we don't have champions to support us, pursuing and achieving our dreams becomes much more difficult.

So many successful people have leveraged a circle of peers, friends and champions who cared about them and supported them in their dreams. When you have people in your life who you trust and who support you, you become mutual champions for each other. And, it is these champions who are there for you during the inevitable peaks and valleys that lie ahead in your journey.

YOUR TURN

1. Take a few minutes to list those individuals who might become potential champions for your journey:

Successful, older adults you already know:

_____

_____

_____

Successful, older adults you don't know (yet!):

_____

_____

_____

Friends or associates you highly respect and who have similar dreams or values:

_____

_____

_____

2. Once you have this list, schedule time in your week to call or email at least two of the names on your list. Explain who you are, why you're contacting them and why you admire them. Ask if they would be willing to meet with you for coffee or lunch. Don't ask them to be your champion just yet—save that for your meeting.

It takes courage to step out in this way—to make that phone call, to send that letter—but you can be assured it might change the trajectory of your life!

DIG DEEPER

READ

- *Never Eat Alone* by Keith Ferazzi
- *The Person Who Changed My Life: Prominent People Recall Their Mentors* by Matilda R. Cuomo
- *Power Mentoring: How Successful Mentors and Proteges Get the Most Out of Their Relationships* by Ellen A. Ensher and Susan E. Murphy

LISTEN

- *Tribe of Mentors* with Tim Ferriss
- **The Mentor List** with David Lewis
- *The John Maxwell Leadership Podcast:* Maximize Your Mentoring

WATCH

- *Cutting Down the Nets: My Bags are Packed* | Jim Valvano—YouTube
- *Good Will Hunting.* Will Hunting, a janitor at MIT., has a gift for mathematics but needs help from a psychologist to find direction in his life.
- *Failure and the Importance of Mentors* | Patrick Boland—TEDxYouth@TheSpire
- *Heroic Journeys Begin with Bold Mentors* | Jeremy Walker—TEDxACU

ACTION STEPS

PREPARE FOR YOUR MEETING

Once you have a meeting scheduled, make sure you come prepared. Plan out the questions you'd like to ask. Make a written list so you don't miss an area you want to discuss. Also, think about your goals for what you'd like to get out of the conversation.

What are the areas that you most want to address in the time you have? You may want to first ask about their own story and career path before you start talking about yourself. Make sure you're as ready to listen as you are to talk.

MAKE A PLAN FOR FOLLOW-UP

Sending a handwritten thank-you note via snail mail to those who take the time to meet with you can be surprisingly effective, especially since so few cards are sent these days. A short, personal note can go a long way toward making your contacts inclined to continue the conversation. Never underestimate the value of a personal touch, and of showing gratitude and initiative.

There is no passion to be found in playing small, settling for a life less than what you are capable of living.

—NELSON MANDELA

Opportunity is missed by most people because it is dressed in overalls and looks like work.

—THOMAS EDISON

Until one is committed, there is hesitancy, the chance to draw back, always ineffectiveness. Concerning all acts of initiative (and creation), there is one elementary truth, the ignorance of which kills countless ideas and splendid plans: that the moment one definitely commits oneself, then Providence moves, too. All sorts of things occur to help one that would never otherwise have occurred. A whole stream of events issues from the decision, raising in one's favor all manner of unforeseen incidents and meetings and material assistance, which no man could have dreamed would have come his way. Whatever you can do, or dream you can do, begin it. Boldness has genius, power and magic in it. Begin it now.

—GOETHE

CHAPTER 5

TAKE THE FIRST STEPS

When I reflect on all the things I've dreamed of doing that never materialized, the lack of results has almost always been because I was simply too hesitant to take that all-important first step.

On the flip side, when I have found the courage to actually take that first action, I've almost always experienced a positive outcome.

For as long as I can remember, I have dreamed of being an entrepreneur. When I was in my early forties, after I had spent many years working for companies that were owned and controlled by others, I found myself envisioning a day when I'd start and run my own education company. This dream had been rattling around in my head for years. I had even revised my vision statement to outline this dream in detail just a few months before I began to seriously consider my options, yet I still wasn't sure that I could actually make that vision happen.

When I finally got the courage to do something about it and take that first action step, I nervously called an investment banker in the education industry to share my idea with him. That phone call was the first step in growing my tiny seed of an idea into the company I run today. Hearing him react positively to my idea and confirm that there was indeed a potential opportunity for me to innovate in the private school arena was all the encouragement I needed to keep moving forward. From there, I ran with it and started taking other actions that helped me build toward my goals.

> What is *one* first action step you can take this week toward your goals?

CHOOSE YOUR FIRST STEP

You likely have a big dream, too. The most important thing to remember is that the difference between an idea always remaining a dream or becoming a reality is a person's willingness to write it down and take that first action step. Your first step, like mine, doesn't have to be huge. It could simply be telling a friend, a spouse or a partner about what you envision. It could be that you start doing initial research.

Regardless of the specific action you choose to take initially, the important thing is to simply START. Once you do, you'll be surprised at how much energy you get from it and how much easier steps two, three, four and five become.

FIND A FRIENDLY EAR

Sometimes a great first action step is mustering up the courage to simply talk about it. Find a friendly ear to express your thoughts and solicit constructive feedback. A friendly audience might be your family or best friend, or it could be someone you admire who has interest or experience in your field (a champion) and who you believe could offer helpful support and feedback.

For example, when I called that first investment banker about my idea, I knew he had significant expertise in education, but I was also hoping he'd be a friendly audience who would offer advice and encouragement. I look back now and can see how his little bit of positive feedback led me to my next step, which was talking to a second person in the industry.

Following that, I put together an outline of my concept. Then, I created a PowerPoint presentation which I tweaked along the way as I received feedback from others. Next, I made appointments to talk with potential investors. By taking each of these steps over time, I became more confident and more committed to my dream. With a little bit of courage and a few well-placed phone calls to people I had networked with in the past, my idea moved from one that was fairly vague and just taking shape to one that became clearer and more precise.

Who might provide a friendly ear to share your idea? Make a plan to connect with that person.

BREAK EVERYTHING INTO MANAGEABLE CHUNKS

Your dream might seem like a big idea that's impossible to reach. Big ideas and big visions are energizing, but they can also be scary and intimidating. The secret to accomplishing even the biggest goals is breaking them down into small, manageable chunks.

For example, imagine that one of the goals on your lifetime bucket list is to hike a significant portion of the

Appalachian Trail. What are the first steps you need to take in order to set foot on that trail?

First, you need to research how long it is, where to begin on the section you want to hike, how to physically navigate the trail via the network of markers and maps that are available, and the best times of the year to begin your journey. Next, you'll need to determine the kind of equipment you'll need—from clothing, boots and socks to cooking utensils to rain gear and shelter options. You'll also want to study how other individuals have managed to get food and supplies to predetermined drop points along the way, and where they were able to stop to rest and refuel.

> Once you've taken your first action step, begin mapping out what you think might be steps two, three and four. Write as many steps down as you can think of. Doing this will help you break your big dream down into smaller steps that feel more manageable.

Finally, your best and most insightful input will be from others who are passionate about sharing their stories because they love the Appalachian Trail and are eager to advise others on how to successfully navigate the trail. These are the friends and experts who will be able to best counsel you on how to train for the challenges of the trail, the best gear to take with you, the kind of support you'll need and the best way to prepare for success in reaching your goal.

Hiking a significant portion of the Appalachian Trail is definitely an intimidating prospect. If you never get off the couch and just let the idea rattle around in your head, you will certainly never achieve your goal. And without the proper preparation, achieving your goal is highly unlikely as well.

Could you put on your old, beat-up running shoes, throw food in a backpack, travel to the trailhead, and just start walking? Certainly, you could. But the best way to ensure your success will be to first take steps to prepare for a successful journey. Regardless, taking the initiative to move forward in research is the first step toward taking that literal first step on the trail.

The moral of the story is that all great accomplishments start with that all-important decision to just get started, to take that first single action to get the ball rolling. For me, it started with a single phone call. From there, I could ask myself, "What's the next step? . . . And the next?" Breaking it down helps us avoid getting overwhelmed by the enormity of the dream and what it might take to get there. By taking one step at a time, everything becomes more manageable and the dream becomes more realistic with each step taken.

PERFECTION IS THE ENEMY OF ACTION

If you think everything has to be perfect before you move forward with your plans, you'll never take action. It's easy to let the fear of failure or of not being perfect stop you in your tracks. But none of us can expect that our first actions will be perfect actions. To imagine that is completely unrealistic.

In fact, when you're first starting out, you're unlikely to have a well-defined game plan. You'll need to try and fail and learn and then try and fail and learn some more. It is through these failures that you'll become smarter, better, stronger and more successful. Failures and setbacks along the way help you build the resilience that is critically important to ultimately getting where you want to go.

After my initial call with the investment banker, I moved ahead with my plan to raise money to start my company by talking to and presenting to at least fifty investors—and forty-seven of them said no. But with every "no" along the way, I adjusted my business plan, tweaked my presentation and got better as I worked through the challenges. If I had simply stopped after talking to only a few prospective investors, I would never have built Fusion Education Group, and I'd be in an entirely different spot today.

It's important to be thorough and do your research. Talk to others to gain insight. But don't let the fear of making a few wrong decisions or not having every detail firmed up stop you from moving forward.

HARD WORK BEATS TALENT OVER TIME

It's sometimes easy to wonder if you have "what It takes;" if you have enough talent or skills to make your dreams happen. All of us have these moments of uncertainty. However, it's been my experience that hard work always beats talent over the long haul.

Everyone has the ability to eventually master a skill through hard work and effort. Talent might offer an edge initially, but it's the grit and determination to do the hard work over the long term that makes you successful. While natural talent is important, it's more important to have a mindset that embraces the importance of hard work and commits to overcoming unhelpful habits and beliefs.

This short research summary provides excellent insight:

Dr. Benjamin Bloom of the University of Chicago conducted a five-year study of leading artists, athletes and scholars based on anonymous interviews with the top 20 performers in various fields, as well as with their friends, families and teachers. He wanted to discover the common characteristics of these achievers that led to their tremendous successes.

He said, "We expected to find tales of great natural gifts. We didn't find that at all. Their mothers often said it was another child who had the greater talents."

What Bloom did find were stories of hard work and dedication: the swimmer who performed laps for two hours every morning before school and the pianist who practiced several hours a day for years.

Bloom's research exemplifies my point: hard work—not great talent—is what leads to extraordinary achievements. It's quite often not the most talented individual who becomes the star of the team or who becomes the bestselling author. Rather, it's the one who is filled with determination and dedicates the long hours it will take to perfect their craft, who decides to make their passion a priority, and who is willing to go "all in" to achieve those goals who finishes first.

OVERCOME FEAR: DON'T GIVE UP BEFORE YOU BEGIN

It is sometimes tempting to hold back; to not give everything we have to a dream because we're afraid. We rationalize to ourselves that it is easier to not give one hundred percent because if we fail, we have an "out." We can then simply tell ourselves and others that things didn't work out because we didn't really try all that hard in the first place. Or, we can let ourselves off the hook by telling ourselves it really wasn't that important to us anyway. These are convenient excuses, born out of fear and insecurities, that never lead to success.

The truth is, there are no guarantees. You could work your hardest, and your plans could still fail. It has happened to me plenty of times (as you can see in this book). But the only way you'll ever know whether or not you can make your dreams a reality is by trying, by taking action. If you take yourself out of the game before you try, failure is guaranteed. As I frequently told my kids when they were playing little-league baseball, "If you don't swing the bat, you are one hundred percent sure of not getting a hit."

A life spent wondering "What if?" and "What might have been?" is far worse than any one failure.

MY STORY

I was never a morning person. In college, I never had a class before 9 or 10 a.m. because I disliked getting up early. In my early career, I would hit the snooze button multiple times before finally getting out of bed. So it makes sense that as I moved into my career, exercise was certainly not part of my morning routine.

However, a few colleagues in my YPO peer group had mastered the art of exercising in the morning and encouraged me to consider doing the same. At first, I decided it just wasn't for me, and, frankly, I completely dismissed the idea. Eventually, though, I decided to at least try it once. I woke up early that next morning, and after working out, I noticed I felt better and had more energy that day. Slowly, I committed to exercising one morning at a time. It took me an entire year to build that habit. At first, I would exercise only once or twice a week, but today, many years later, I exercise five to six mornings a week. The habit has built upon itself and become stronger over time. Today, my morning exercise is the key to starting my day off on the right foot.

The same pattern followed when a friend, a frequent marathoner, encouraged me to run a marathon over a dinner one night. At first, I got excited about the idea, but then the enormity of the goal set in and I didn't do anything about it. I had been a periodic runner for quick exercise and to stay in shape, but never more than a few miles at a time. Running 26.2 miles simply seemed out of reach for me. The idea continued to gnaw at me though. Eventually, my friend suggested to just look online for marathons that might at least be of interest (that critical "first step"!).

We found one in Cincinnati—my hometown—and the idea of returning home to run a marathon started to intrigue me and I committed to it. So first, I started running for exercise to get back in shape again. I ran three miles. After a few weeks, I pushed myself to five. Then I told myself if I could run five miles, I certainly could do six. I slowly built my endurance, and as I moved into longer training runs of fifteen, eighteen, and more than twenty miles, my friend and I ran together as we both trained for marathons taking place at approximately the same time.

Before I knew it, at age forty-three, I had gone from rejecting the idea to completing my first marathon in my hometown of Cincinnati.

This is a key part in the process of reaching any difficult goal or dream. We start with an interest or idea that seems daunting or out of reach. We often dismiss it initially, but we continue to think about it, see the benefits and become interested enough to commit to it. But, despite that commitment, we are not really committed.

We are only partially committed until we actually take that first step by doing a bit of research, or going on that first run, or making a call or setting a meeting. After that, we move to the next step. Eventually, these first steps build on themselves, create momentum and help us fully embrace accomplishing the goal. From there, we might push ourselves to take an even bigger leap.

Practicing this process—of taking that one first step and then a second step—teaches us that it is possible to get beyond our doubts and fears and move toward the kind of limitless life we've imagined. Setting a big goal is worthless unless and until we take those first critical action steps. Inaction significantly multiplies fear and hesitancy. Taking positive action unleashes the tremendous human power within all of us.

The marketing guru Seth Godin once described a potential opportunity like a blank check in your wallet. In one of his great blogs, he said:

> A check in your wallet does you very little good. It represents opportunity, sure, but not action.
>
> Most of us are carrying around a check, an opportunity to make an impact, to do the work we're capable of, to ship the art that would make a difference.
>
> No, the world isn't fair, and most people don't get all the chances they deserve. There are barriers due to income, to race, to social standing, and to education, and they are inexcusable and must fall. But the check remains, now more than ever. The

opportunity to step up and to fail ... until we succeed is greater now than it has ever been.

As Martin Luther King Junior spoke about a half a lifetime ago,

We are now faced with the fact, my friends, that tomorrow is today. We are confronted with *the fierce urgency of now.* In this unfolding conundrum of life and history, there is such a thing as being too late. Procrastination is still the thief of time. Life often leaves us standing bare, naked, and dejected with a lost opportunity. The tide in the affairs of men does not remain at flood—it ebbs. We may cry out desperately for time to pause in her passage, but time is adamant to every plea and rushes on. Over the bleached bones and jumbled residues of numerous civilizations are written the pathetic words, "Too late."

January 17, 2011

YOUR TURN

The first step in facing our fears is acknowledging they exist. List any activities you've been afraid to try or goals you've avoided setting because you're worried you might fail:

_____

_____

_____

_____

_____

Now, list the specific fears or concerns that would be holding you back from trying these activities or pursuing your goals:

_____

_____

_____

_____

_____

DIG DEEPER

READ

- *Outliers: The Story of Success* by Malcolm Gladwell
- *Poke the Box: When Was the Last Time You Did Something for the First Time?* by Seth Godin
- *Educated: A Memoir* by Tara Westover

LISTEN

- *How I Built This* with Guy Raz—Springfree Trampoline: Keith Alexander & Steve Holmes
- *The Startup Story* with James McKinney

WATCH

- *The Most Important Decision is Getting Started* | Laura Behrens Wu—YouTube. The twenty-six-year-old CEO and Co-Founder of Shippo built her company after meeting with 125 investors and receiving 115 rejections! Her story is one of persistence and using failure as an opportunity to grow and improve along the way.
- *Brittany Runs a Marathon.* An overweight woman in New York City sets out only to lose weight but eventually completes the city's annual marathon.
- *How to Achieve Your Most Ambitious Goals* | Stephen Duneier—TEDxTucson

----

ACTION STEPS

Once we've acknowledged and named our fears, we can face them, one by one, by taking action. The smallest step forward is often the most important step!

Write down a dream or goal or activity that's important to you and list three immediate actions you can take to start down the path. Make sure these actions are manageable, easily accomplished and not overly intimidating.

Goal:

_____

_____

_____

_____

First action steps:

_____

_____

_____

_____

Set a date to complete each of these small actions and hold yourself accountable by sharing your list with a friend or champion.

The truth is, everything that has happened in my life . . . that I thought was a crushing event at the time, has turned out for the better.

—WARREN BUFFET

I can accept failure, but I can't accept not trying.

—MICHAEL JORDAN

Everyone has the desire to succeed, but very few people have the courage to fail.

—MANOJ SAXENA,
GENERAL MANAGER OF WATSON SOLUTIONS AT IBM

Most people never pick up the phone and call; most people never ask. And that's what separates sometimes the people that do things from the people that just dream about them. You've gotta act, and you've gotta be willing to fail, and you've gotta be willing to crash and burn, with people on the phone, with starting a company, or whatever. If you're afraid of failing, you won't get very far.

—STEVE JOBS

Every person who has ever achieved anything has been knocked down many times. But all of them picked themselves up and kept going.

—WANGARI MAATHAI,
NOBEL PEACE PRIZE-WINNING ENVIRONMENTALIST

CHAPTER 6

FAIL OFTEN

There are many stories of well-known individuals who have attributed their success to repeated failure.

- J. K. Rowling, the author of the Harry Potter book series, was a single mother and nearly homeless before her repeated attempts to find a publisher for her first book were rewarded with an acceptance letter.
- Steve Jobs, one of the founders of Apple and its renowned CEO, was fired from the company he created. After finding success in other business ventures, he came back to Apple as it was on its last leg, saved it and led it to become the most valuable company in the world at the time of his death.
- Michael Jordan, in a well-known Nike advertisement, talks about how many times he was called on to take the winning shot in games and missed. He attributes those failures as his driving motivation to continue to succeed.

- Abraham Lincoln was a small-town attorney who ran for several elected positions and failed time and time again. His failures affected him deeply, and he even endured a nervous breakdown at one point. But he was able to find the courage and motivation to persist in taking advantage of opportunities presented to him and was eventually elected to be America's sixteenth president.

- Thomas Edison had an unusual take on his repeated attempts to create different inventions, saying, "I haven't failed. I've just found ten thousand ways that won't work."

No one likes to fail. Every one of us, at some level, is afraid of making mistakes. Failure is embarrassing, it can leave us feeling exposed, and it never feels good.

Is there a successful person in your life you admire? Ask them about not only their successes, but also their failures along the way. You will be surprised what you learn from them and the wisdom they'll be willing to share!

When I was cut from my high school basketball team, I was devastated. To add to my humiliation, some of my best friends made the team when I didn't. It was a big blow to my ego at the time, and I even considered going back to my old school after being cut. I thought about giving up or trying another sport.

Looking back, I can see how that particular failure provided one of my earliest and most enduring learning experiences. By trying out for the team, yet not making it, I felt knocked down. But I also learned that failure is not final. I realized it could push me to try harder, to find a different path to success, to become better, and, in this case, eventually to succeed.

Through that early experience, I learned to view failure differently by understanding that it can also be a significant learning experience and generate personal growth. Not making the team taught me that failure isn't something I should fear, but that it's actually something I should embrace. It sounds counterintuitive, but it's true and an extremely important concept. From that one experience as a fourteen-year-old freshman, I learned about not giving up, about the importance of hard work (above and beyond just the "expected" level), about determination and about never leaving future success to chance.

THE COURAGE TO FAIL

No one who decides to pursue a dream arrives there easily. Successful people usually go through any number of failures before achieving their goals. If you study their stories beyond the summary headlines of success and dig deeply, you'll likely discover how hard they worked and how many times they stumbled along the way to get to their dreams. When we admire someone's current accomplishments, we often think of only the successful person they are today, but rarely grasp the trials and tribulations they overcame on the long journey to get there.

To really pursue your unique vision for your life, you need to be "all-in." And that means having the courage to risk failure. If you think about it, the people who haven't failed in life are usually those who've never tried very hard. They've never pushed themselves to move outside their comfort zone. Constrained by fear and the worry of what might go wrong, their life has likely remained small because they've been unwilling to step outside of the box to explore the larger world around them and discover their own potential.

People who are constrained by a desire to avoid failure often hesitate to try new things. This a failure of omission. By protecting themselves in this way, they settle for "good enough" and never really attempt to achieve their dreams or goals. They often become small-minded and insular instead of remaining curious and open-minded about what they might accomplish.

WHAT HAPPENS WHEN YOU FAIL?

Fact: If you are living a bold, meaningful life, you are not always going to succeed. Dreams will fall short, ideas will collapse and your best will not always be enough. Even though you can learn a lot from failure, it never feels good. It's often surrounded by a dark period in which you question yourself, your worth or your dreams. Even when you get up and dust yourself off, it still hurts.

Think of a recent failure that you've experienced, and instead of focusing on the negative, ask: "What does this failure make possible? What does it teach me about myself? What did I learn from it that will help me in the future?"

As I mentioned in chapter 1, I was a co-owner of a successful consulting firm in Boston at age twenty-eight. But after a few years of success, our client base began drying up, and we had to eventually close the business. There I was, "co-owner" of a failed business, with no job and a wife and a new baby to support. It was a dark time for me.

I had to dig deep and choose to not let that failure define me. I had to get up and figure out how to move forward. And it's the very failure of that business, and all the learnings that came with it, that put me on the road toward the work I do today. Although this business failure certainly wasn't part of my original plan, I believed in myself and my long term vision enough that it helped me get out of bed every day and keep pushing my way through those tough circumstances toward my dreams.

RESILIENCE WINS IN THE END

Sometimes failure necessitates taking a step or two back to re-strategize and refocus on your goals before you start climbing again. That Is the essence of resilience—having the ability to pick yourself up after you've been knocked down. It involves refusing to listen to your insecurities and being willing to let go of what's comfortable In order to continue the pursuit of your dreams, even when there are no guarantees.

MY STORY

In my early forties, I found myself doing a lot of soul-searching during my long commutes back and forth to work as the CEO of a healthcare organization. I had taken the position because it seemed like an amazing opportunity, but it wasn't long before I realized I had made a significant failure in judgment. The job was not a good fit, and I was miserable.

I knew I could stay the course and continue working in what looked like a great job from the outside. I was CEO. I made a good living. I was in charge. But I also knew I was unhappy, and deep down, I knew staying would feel like a failure because I was accepting something I knew wasn't right for me.

With the support of my wife, I ultimately decided to resign. What felt like a failure in judgment quickly moved to a much more obvious external failure to my family and friends. I had gone from being a CEO with a lot of respect, great benefits and perks to an unemployed forty-three-year-old now with a fourth child on the way. My whole world and our lifestyle changed dramatically. I no longer had a team to lead or even a place to go to work in the morning, and I felt a deep sense of emptiness. Again, it was a time of considerable soul-searching.

My first inclination was to look for another job. I started interviewing and contacting recruiting firms. But I also knew in my gut that I really wanted to get back into education where I had experienced previous success, and I wanted to start and build a company from scratch. My wife and I had a number of long conversations about whether I should simply focus on finding another job with a consistent income or take a chance and chase my dream. We finally determined that this might be my best (and potentially only) chance to pursue that dream.

Together, we agreed I would take the 2006 calendar year to try to raise the money needed to start a company. If I couldn't do it within that year, I'd move on and look for a different job.

I spent the entire year talking to respected mentors and potential investors about my business idea, and, despite an endless amount of "no's," was finally able to secure the needed capital investment just as that year was coming to a close.

Although I eventually found success in starting the company, it certainly wasn't guaranteed and there were a number of failures along the way and moments of severe doubt. I know just how tempting it is to not make a career switch because the position you're in is comfortable or the money is good.

But comfort is the enemy of making dreams come true. I did not want to wake up some day and wonder, "What if?" Even if I had a successful career otherwise, I would have always known that I had shelved my dreams in the interest of comfort and security.

I don't necessarily think everyone should do what I did and quit their job and live without an income for an extended period of time. But we all can take small steps toward making our dreams a reality. We can reduce the risk by investing time in the evenings or parts of our weekends to develop actionable plans toward pursuing our dreams.

That's why crafting your long-term vision is so important. It can provide the motivational fuel you need to help you determine your next best steps when failures happen and times get tough.

YOUR TURN
WHAT WOULD YOU DO IF YOU WEREN'T AFRAID?

What dream would you pursue if you weren't afraid? Is there something you know you would love to do, but you've allowed fear to stop you from moving ahead and trying?

_____

_____

_____

_____

Sheryl Sandberg, COO of Facebook and author of *Lean In*, gave a university commencement address in 2011 that ended with this challenge: "Please ask yourself: What would I do if I weren't afraid? And then go do it."

It's a question worth asking. Think about it in the coming days and weeks. Journal about it as you imagine what you might want to accomplish. Write down your fears, your questions and your ideas about the "what would I do" answers you come up with. And then find the courage to go for it!

_____

_____

_____

_____

DIG DEEPER

READ

- *Left To Tell* by Immaculee Ilibagiza. This is an inspiring story of a young woman who survived the 1994 Rwandan genocide and is now an author and motivational speaker.
- *Shoe Dog: A Memoir by the Creator of Nike* by Phil Knight
- *Daring Greatly: How the Courage to be Vulnerable Transforms the Way We Live, Love, Parent, and Lead* by Brené Brown

LISTEN

- *The Tim Ferriss Show*
- *Spectacular Failures* by American Public Media
- *How to Fail* with Elizabeth Day

WATCH

- *Why am I even alive?* | Muniba Mazari —YouTube. Mazari, referred to as the Iron Lady of Pakistan, talks about how her life and perspective changed after a car accident left her without the use of her legs.
- *Octavia Spencer's 2017 commencement address* at Kent State University
- *The fringe benefits of failure* | JK Rowling—TED Talk

-- --

ACTION STEPS

List what you believe are some of your biggest past failures. Then take a look at the list and note: What did you learn from each of these failures? Are there ways they made you better or stronger?

Failures and lessons:

_____

_____

_____

_____

_____

Growth as a result:

_____

_____

_____

_____

_____

It's helpful to know we're not the only ones who experience failure. In fact, many successful people have also experienced spectacular failures. Take just a few minutes to Google other famous people who have failed. Then read more and be inspired by their stories of overcoming their failures.

Courage isn't the absence of fear but rather the decision that something else is more important than fear.

—FRANKLIN D. ROOSEVELT

The person who follows the crowd will usually go no further than the crowd. The person who walks alone is likely to find himself in places no one has ever seen before.

—ALBERT EINSTEIN

Discomfort is the price of admission to a meaningful life.

—SUSAN DAVID

CHAPTER 7

BE COURAGEOUS

When I quit my job as the leader of a healthcare organization, I didn't know if I could successfully build an education company. While I believed in my abilities, I also knew nothing was a sure thing. I could work my hardest at raising the capital I needed, yet I could still be unsuccessful. We could start the company but still fail down the road. There were no guarantees.

Despite these fears, I still found the courage to go after my dream. It's the reason I'm able to do work I love today, and it's why courage is so important to a limitless life.

Courage is not about being fearless in the face of a scary situation. It is the willingness to move forward or take action—*despite* your fear. It's about finding the will to bridge the gap between where you are and where you want to be, even when getting there seems daunting.

Over the years, I've learned that no matter how many times I act courageously, I can still count on two things:

1. I will be afraid.
2. I need to be brave enough to act anyway, even if it's difficult or means breaking away from other people's expectations of what I should do.

Having the courage to move ahead despite fear is always hard work and is a never-ending growth process.

THE COURAGE TO MOVE OUT OF YOUR COMFORT ZONE

We have all likely heard this commonly quoted definition of insanity: doing the same thing over and over again, yet expecting a different result. This applies to building courage as well. If you never get out of your comfort zone, and instead continue surrounding yourself with the same people, the same perspectives and the same norms, you'll never stretch yourself in ways that encourage you to take big leaps in your life. You'll continue to play it safe, and you'll never learn to be courageous.

Is there a situation in your life now that requires courage to move forward? What might it look like to take specific action— despite your fear?

Presidential Medal of Honor winner Desmond Doss was a conscientious objector who was drafted into World War II and required to serve in some capacity despite his beliefs. Initially, he was the object of ridicule from other soldiers for his staunch religious convictions and refusal to carry or use a weapon. Later, however, he was serving as a field medic on the island of Okinawa when his unit came under extreme fire from the Japanese. The unit was trapped on the edge of a cliff, and his fellow soldiers were exposed and being gunned down at an alarming rate. Rather than cower or run, Doss quickly rigged an innovative stretcher using ropes and pulleys to lower his wounded comrades down the cliff where they could be moved away from their forward position and get their injuries treated. A defenseless, unarmed combatant, he risked almost certain death while he took nearly fifty men off the cliff, saving their lives.

This is just one example of possessing relentless courage under extreme conditions. Examples like Desmond Doss can fuel our energy levels and inspire us to move forward in much less treacherous situations.

Courage is important for three reasons:

1. Courage gets you where you want to be

You can do many of the things we've talked about in this book—have big dreams, create your vision, discover your passions and find supportive mentors—but if you never find the courage to believe in yourself and take that first step, you'll never get where you want to go. You must be willing to leave what is secure and comfortable in order to allow room for everything else to happen. You have to be willing to break away from so called, "friends," who want to dismiss your dreams or hold you back.

2. Courage fuels the next time

Taking action when you know something is failure-proof doesn't require courage. But attempting something, even when knowing you might fail, is the key to learning that there is no shame in failure. Every failure is simply an opportunity to realize that it is possible to get up after you fall, learn from the experience and course correct. Many great people have experienced failure and recovered. Like them, you can learn from your experiences and do better next time. Courage is what fuels the impetus to get back up and do better the "next time."

3. Courage builds on itself

The more we display and practice courage, the more we gain confidence. And the more we gain confidence, the less fearful we become. Any individual's personal and professional lives inevitably present challenges and opportunities that seem daunting. Facing each of these proactively, one by one, can help you literally practice having courage in the face of these challenges. The more you find success in using your courage to build toward your next step, the greater the chance you'll learn to see how resilient you really are.

HOW CAN I DEVELOP COURAGE?

1. Practice

The best way to be more courageous is to keep trying. Practice exercising courage in both small and big ways and you'll soon find that fear gets a bit smaller each time—although it never completely goes away.

2. Surround yourself with courageous people

Think about the five people you interact with most often. Are they courageous? Do they take risks out of their comfort zones to progress toward their goals? Spending time with others who encourage us to step out of our comfort zones is essential. When we find a group of people who live courageously, we feed off of their strength and learn that we can begin to encourage others to be courageous as well.

3. Know what you value

When you know what's important to you—the things you believe are worth standing up for—it's a bit easier to find the courage to take action. In the previous story of Desmond Doss, he stood by his values and acted in accordance with them despite constant initial ridicule from his peers. He was able to be courageous in a way that didn't compromise his deeply held values, and he succeeded well beyond what anyone would have expected of him.

Which of these five ideas resonates with you most? What could you start working on today to develop more courage in your life choices?

4. Be self-accountable

We are in no way entitled to success in life. No one owes you a job or a better opportunity. Your destiny will be a result of what *you* do, so learn early that blaming your shortcomings on others isn't going to lead to success. Pointing fingers is never productive. The only way to finding personal success is understanding that you are the only one who is going to be able to move you toward your dreams and then finding ways to hold yourself accountable to take those actions.

5. Get comfortable with failure

Failure is the best teacher any of us could have. So, don't be afraid of it. Be smart about what you pursue, but embrace failures when you can learn from them.

MY STORY

Back In 2013, I had an idea to create a military celebration and thanksgiving event for veterans in my city. I saw a need, so I let it roll around in my head for a while. I finally wrote it down as a goal. It then sat on my goals list for a couple of years before I said anything to anyone about it.

I knew I had no military background or experience, and I wasn't even sure how to pull off such a celebration. I only had a desire to show appreciation for all those who had sacrificed so much and served our country. Would anyone come? Would people even think it was a good idea? What if there were already events like this out there? What if no one would serve on a planning committee with me? What if the event wasn't well-received, and I couldn't find people to support it?

Fear is what kept me from moving forward.

But after periodically reviewing my goals list and being reminded that I hadn't done anything with this idea yet, I found the courage to take my first step: talking with a friend about it over lunch. I told him about my vision and how I felt our area veterans would benefit from something like this, and I asked if he'd be interested in helping me figure out how to create the event. He said yes!

That single action gave me the courage to discuss the concept with another friend and then another friend. From there, we put together a steering committee to help create the plan and take the actions necessary to realize our goal, and the event launched about a year and a half later in 2016. Today, the Armed Forces Thanksgiving is a sold-out event attended by nearly 750 people each year. It has raised a significant amount of money for veteran's support causes across West Michigan, and it also serves as an education event for high school students in the area. The event is now expanding to other cities.

I took inspiration from others who had previously created new charitable events that now, year after year, make a difference in their communities. This helped me find the confidence I needed to take my first step forward. I also know that my previous experiences—when I've practiced pushing past the fear of doing something new or different—helped me find the courage to move forward one bite-sized, manageable step at a time.

It is easy to look back now and see how my courage in the face of a rather daunting idea paid off. But, it's also important to note that it took me two years to even have that first conversation with my friend. Here I was, a fifty-year-old, successful business professional, yet I still struggled with the same basic fears and insecurities we all have when we consider trying something new.

It is another example of how I've learned that developing courage is a journey that builds on itself over time. People do not suddenly become courageous. We don't just suddenly start to act courageously in all situations. We're always growing and learning, and continued practice moves us toward becoming more courageous each time.

I still live with doubts about my ability to achieve my goals and dreams every day. We all do. Courage comes from finding a way to act *despite* having those fears.

YOUR TURN

Consider this quote from Sheryl Sandberg again in light of what you've learned in this chapter: "Please ask yourself: What would I do if I weren't afraid? And then go do it."

What are two first action steps you could take this week toward being more courageous in your life?

First action steps:

_____

_____

_____

_____

_____

_____

_____

_____

_____

DIG DEEPER
READ

- *Unbroken: A World War II Story of Survival, Resilience and Redemption* by Laura Hillenbrand
- *The Courage Habit: How to Accept Your Fears, Release the Past, and Live Your Courageous Life* by Kate Swoboda and Bari Tessler
- *The Courage Challenge Workbook: Creating a Culture of Courage* by Cindy Solomon

LISTEN

- *Akimbo:* A Podcast from Seth Godin
- *Andy Molinsky: The Psychology of Getting Out of Your Comfort Zone* on The Unmistakable Mindset

WATCH

- *Invictus.* This recounts the true story of Nelson Mandela's courage to believe that one simple idea could unite an entire country.
- *Brené Brown: The Call to Courage*—Netflix. In this 2019 documentary, Brené Brown discusses what it takes to choose courage over comfort in today's culture.
- *How to Build Your Courage* | Cindy Solomon— TEDxSonomaCounty

---

ACTION STEPS

Where does a lack of courage show up in your life? Think about your current friends and peers:

List those who have big goals:

List those who might be holding you back (intentionally or unintentionally) from pursuing your dreams and setting bigger goals in your life:

Revisit your past failures and challenges. Who or what have you blamed? Think deeply about how you could move away from your past struggles, challenges or mistreatments that are holding you back today and how you can move toward a more self-accountable future where you write your own success. How might you choose to handle future challenges differently?

The greatest accomplishment is not in never falling, but in rising again after you fall.

—VINCE LOMBARDI

It's not how many times you get knocked down,
It's how many times you get back up.

It's not how many failures you experience,
It's how many you learn and grow from.

It's not how many goals you set and begin to pursue,
It's how many you continue pursuing despite obstacles.

It's not about finding the easy route when things get tough,
It's a willingness to take that next step up the
mountain, even when it's steep and treacherous.

It's about knowing life won't always be easy.
You will struggle.
You will fail.
Expect it.
Plan to learn and grow from every failure.
And, most importantly, GET BACK UP.

—PETE RUPPERT

CHAPTER 8

NEVER, EVER GIVE UP

If you continue to build courage throughout your life and take each next step with grit, determination and a knowledge that failures along the way are part of the process, you will eventually come out on the other side successful.

A few years ago, National Geographic came out with a documentary following the courageous exploits of Alex Honnold, a professional mountain climber and a man of incredible courage and resilience. This documentary, called *Free Solo*, details Honnold's relentless preparation in his superhuman attempt to conquer something that had never been accomplished before—scaling the sheer, 900-meter granite rock face of Yosemite's El Capitan without the help of ropes or other safety climbing gear.

The documentary is a fascinating, inspiring and even terrifying study of one man's dogged determination to use his expertise and push his physical limits to the breaking point in the pursuit of a goal that has consumed him for years. Watching Honnold in this documentary epitomizes the "never, ever give up" message in this chapter, as he prepares himself relentlessly for the attempt and is turned back on his first try. Watching him regroup and summon the physical and mental stamina to make a second, successful attempt is both harrowing and, ultimately, amazing.

KNOWING WHEN TO PIVOT

Although I'm a huge believer in never giving up, I also know it doesn't necessarily mean climbing blindly up a mountain and never looking around to see what's happening. Before he ever attempted to scale El Capitan without safety gear, Honnold spent hours, days, and even weeks on the rock face of the obstacle with his fellow climbers. He carefully mapped out his route, writing down his observations in his strategy journal and considering even the smallest details before he set out to try. But despite months of intensive physical and mental preparation and a detailed execution plan, he had to come off the mountain in the early stages of his first attempt.

Honnold had to consider all of the potential factors that he would face on his climb. The same is true when we consider the path we're taking toward reaching our own goals. Is there a potential personal or professional storm ahead? Are there any factors that constitute a steep drop-off you need to avoid at all costs? Do you have a clear picture of every financial consideration to factor in along the way? These are some of the variables that are important to consider as you move along your journey.

We can all expect to struggle at times. But disappointment is also our greatest teacher, so it is important to stop and evaluate challenges during those times to ensure we are still chasing the right objectives—and that we are still on the right path.

Part of our opportunity in life is being able to learn from the obstacles we encounter and evaluate when to pivot along the way, gathering important feedback to inform the journey to our ultimate goal. We may even find that our goal needs to change as we learn more during our journey.

As Honnold discovered, you may find you have to go down in order to go up again, and you'll have to be willing to make those course corrections along the way. The end goal you ultimately achieve may look a bit different from the original vision you laid out when you first started your process. But, like Honnold proved, ultimate success combines knowing when to pivot with a "never give up" commitment. This is all part of growing and learning to not just "throw in the towel" when times get tough. There is a way to get there, find it!

TYING IT ALL TOGETHER

Each chapter I have presented in this book so far—winning the battle in your head, finding a passion, dreaming big, finding a mentor, taking action, failing often and being courageous—are ladder steps to this chapter. Each step is designed to lay the foundation for the steps that follow and to provide a simple, overall framework for you to move forward with the vision, knowledge and encouragement to truly never, ever give up, despite the certain difficulties or setbacks.

MY STORY

Being enrolled in the DePauw University honors business program meant that I had the tremendous opportunity to take part in a paid, semester-long business internship during my junior year. In order to participate in this program, I had to maintain a minimum GPA—a requirement that I didn't always achieve.

At the end of my sophomore year, I received a letter from the program letting me know that because my grades had fallen below the minimum threshold, I was now on probation and would be unable to take part in the prestigious internship program during my junior year. This meant that at best, if my grades improved over the next year and I was taken off probation, I would have to pursue an internship during my senior year. Being off campus during my final year of college was something I definitely wanted to avoid.

I sent a letter to the program and appealed their decision. I was eventually granted a hearing with the board and went before the program leaders, the professors and the director of the program. I presented my case, listened to their feedback, answered their questions and, after much deliberation, they agreed that, if my grades improved by the end of fall midterms, I could then interview for any spring-semester internships that might still be available.

However, I really wanted to work with David Morehead, about whom I've written earlier in the book. He was a successful entrepreneur in Dallas, Texas from whom I thought I could learn a great deal about starting and leading a business. Unfortunately, David was visiting my school to interview candidates in September, which was well before I could prove my midterm grades and officially interview for any potential internships. So, before his visit, I wrote him a long, handwritten letter explaining my probationary status but emphasizing why I really wanted to intern with him specifically. I told him that, although I wasn't eligible to interview, I would love the opportunity to meet him during his visit if he was willing.

As a result of that personal letter, he said, "I need to meet this kid." While David was on campus, he arranged to meet me for an interview anyway, which eventually led to him offering me an internship (subject to me getting my grades up, of course).

As I mentioned earlier, David went on to become a lifelong mentor and champion.

Appearing in front of the board, advocating for myself and pursuing an interview with David is clearly not as extreme as an El Capitan experience. However, it is just one, simple but powerful example of how persistence, never giving up and finding a different path can pay off in the short and long term. You know what happens when you simply give up and walk away. That's obvious. But you never know all the positive things that might happen when you simply decide to never, ever give up.

YOUR TURN

Is there a place in your life today where you feel you are stuck or want to give up? Think about that area and take the time to journal about it.

Areas I'm stuck:

_____

_____

_____

_____

Is there anything you have learned that can inform your next steps for moving forward in these situations? Do you need to pivot, as I did when my grades slipped in college? Get creative in thinking about ways you can use what you've learned so far to not give up and to keep moving toward your goals.

Learning and opportunities to pivot:

_____

_____

_____

_____

_____

DIG DEEPER

READ

- *The Power of Habit: Why We Do What We Do in Life and Business* by Charles Duhigg
- *Superbetter: A Revolutionary Approach to Getting Stronger, Happier, Braver and More Resilient—Powered by the Science of Games* by Jane McGonigal. Also check out her TED talk and corresponding smartphone app.
- *The Resilience Breakthrough: 27 Tools for Turning Adversity into Action* by Christian Moore
- *Executive Thinking: The Dream, the Vision, the Mission Achieved* by Leslie L. Kossoff
- *Endurance: Shackelton's Incredible Voyage* by Alfred Lansing. How all 28 crew members survive a two-year ordeal after being shipwrecked In Antarctica.

LISTEN

- *Road to Resilience by Mount Sinai Health System—* The Power of Optimism
- *How I Built This with Guy Raz—*Outdoor Voices: Tyler Haney
- *How I Built This with Guy Raz* "How I Built Resilience" Series. Guy talks with founders and entrepreneurs about how they navigate the COVID turbulent times.

WATCH

- *Free Solo—*National Geographic documentary. Get ready for a breathtaking experience!
- *Rudy.* Rudy had always been told that he was too small and not talented enough to play college football. But he is

determined to overcome the odds and fulfill his dream of playing for Notre Dame.

- *The Pursuit of Happyness.* This compelling autobiographical film follows entrepreneur Chris Gardener's journey from homelessness to success in the financial industry.
- *Overcoming Hopelessness* | Nick Vujicic—TEDxNoviSad
- *Sheryl Sandberg's 2016 commencement address* at UC Berkeley

ACTION STEPS

List ideas you have to find inspiration for staying on track during tough times or when facing difficult obstacles. Think about how you might be able to pivot and discover new ways to approach those obstacles so they feel more surmountable. Rather than simply giving up on a goal, how can you re-strategize and find a different path?

Find your own inspiration for never giving up. Study other people's stories of overcoming long odds to achieve their dreams. What about them and their experience might help you keep going?

Instead of wondering when your next vacation is, maybe you should set up a life you don't need to escape from.

—SETH GODIN

For what it's worth . . . it's never too late, or in my case too early, to be whoever you want to be. There's no time limit. Start whenever you want. You can change or stay the same. There are no rules to this thing. We can make the best or the worst of it. I hope you make the best of it. I hope you see things that startle you. I hope you feel things you've never felt before. I hope you meet people who have a different point of view. I hope you live a life you're proud of, and if you're not, I hope you have the courage to start over again.

—F. SCOTT FITZGERALD

I don't know anyone who on their deathbed said, "Gee, I wish I'd spent more time at the office."

—PETER LYNCH

CHAPTER 9

LIVE

A recent article posted by Christina DesMarais on Inc.com is titled "Science Says You'll Regret Being Too Busy for Friends." It's about the importance of making time and being deliberate about finding balance in your life. DesMarais writes:

> Mentally scroll to the end of your life. What will be your biggest regrets? The statistics are there, thanks to researchers who have asked the question.
>
> Top regrets tend to center on relationships and work, although people describe their regrets about relationships more strongly than their jobs and other nonsocial parts of their lives. According to Neal Roese, professor of marketing at the Kellogg School of Management at Northwestern University, who conducted research on the subject, people most regret not having, losing or the low quality of their social connections. And while romantic

relationships ranked highest, with family close behind, friendships also ranked near the top in frequency of regrets. In essence, people often know how important it is to invest in love and family, but friendships are easier to let slide.

Sometimes, when we are laser-focused on our goals and making our mark on the world, the relentless activity can become all-encompassing. In pursuit of a good life, we can sometimes forget to enjoy what is right in front of us. We move through life from event to event, activity to activity and meeting to meeting, but we often forget to be present in our own life.

One way to address this potential trap is to consider how you might also apply the first eight chapters of this book to your personal life. Think about how you could be more courageous in your relationships and with your family. Make time for cultivating your personal passions. Look for life mentors or find ways you can *be* a champion for others, including your friends.

Prioritizing family relationships and friendships and taking time out of our stressed-out, uber-busy lives to restore and recharge is essential. Achieving this balance is extremely important. Experiencing success in one area of life to the detriment of who you are as a whole person is simply not worth it. The most successful people in life are those who work at staying balanced and succeeding in all areas, not just professionally.

Below are just a few simple things I've learned along the way to help me get the most of this amazing gift called "life":

1. Try new things

Do things outside of the norm for you. Try new activities. Get involved in organizations outside of your career and find ways to expand your world. Breaking from your normal, day-to-day reality also promotes creativity. Like the military tribute my colleagues and I established, getting involved in something new will often push you outside your comfort zone where you meet new people, learn new things and expand your horizons.

2. Explore

See the world. Travel. Make plans to add unique destinations or unique experiences to your bucket list. If you can't afford to travel, find new places to visit in your own hometown or home state. Do some online research to discover unique experiences or unique destinations near you. So often, we have great places right near us that we never take advantage of. Don't get stuck doing the same things with the same people week after week and month after month.

One of the great things about creating a bucket list is you write down a list of things you want to experience or do in your lifetime. Writing things down dramatically increases the chances of them coming true. So, write down all those great ideas and seek out new experiences, even if they are just in your own city for now. Find a great hiking trail, take a picturesque bike ride, visit museums, zoos, aquariums and restaurants.

3. Find adventure

There is so much to see and experience in the world and in your local community. Let your curiosity lead you for a day, a weekend or an entire week and see where it takes you.

4. Have fun

Always make time for the people and the things you enjoy. Engage in activities that light you up. Implement regular times for play in your week—alone, with family and with friends.

5. Read, read, read

Spending hours scrolling through social media or playing games on your phone is an enormous waste of valuable time. Put down your screens and read widely, including books of interest, biographies, fiction and nonfiction. Reading is a great way to challenge yourself, broaden your vocabulary and knowledge, fire your imagination and even increase your intelligence. It is amazing what you can learn from another person's story. So many people effectively stop reading books after high school or college. The reading they do complete is limited to work information, social media and quick articles found on the Internet. Break free from the seductive habit of TV and phones and find the amazing world and profound benefits of consistently reading books. There is so much to entertain us and educate us within the pages. To put it bluntly, smart people read lots of books.

6. Find balance

Make an effort to find balance in your life between work and play. Achieving professional success doesn't mean much if you can't find personal success as well. So, commit to being a successful and well-balanced adult. Make sure your goals also address your desires to be a winner as a spouse, partner, friend, daughter, son or parent.

MY STORY

One of my best influences in this area has been my wife, Jess. She has been instrumental in helping me to learn this last step—to live.

Each year, no matter how busy we are, Jess ensures our family takes time out to go on a unique vacation. She makes sure we start discussing options and dates early, typically leads the research of various locations and helps finalize the agenda and details. On each vacation, we try to visit new destinations, create new experiences and have fun as a family.

It doesn't matter if it's a far-away location for a week or something closer for only a few days—we've certainly done both. What is important is that we intentionally take time out to enjoy the world around us and learn new things. By prioritizing this part of our lives, she has helped us create fun experiences and many great family memories (and helped me stay more balanced in my own life).

It can be so easy to convince ourselves that we are too busy or can't afford to take time out of our hectic, day-to-day schedules. But taking time to relax and recharge can often give us the breather we need to boost our creativity or provide the bigger-picture perspective we're missing when we're stuck just moving from day-to-day, meeting-to-meeting.

By learning to prioritize family time and balancing work and play in this way, my life has certainly been enriched, both personally and professionally.

YOUR TURN

Review the list above and decide on one thing under each heading that you could implement yet this week or in the coming month to help you live your life more fully. Make a conscious choice to move in that direction and share it with others who can help you make some of these things happen!

Try new things:

Explore:

Find adventure:

Have fun:

Read, read, read:

Find balance:

DIG DEEPER

READ

- *The Third Door: The Wild Quest to Uncover How the World's Most Successful People Launched Their Careers* by Alex Banayan
- *Leading with Cultural Intelligence: The New Secret to Success* by David Livermore
- *Dare to Lead: Brave Work. Tough Conversations. Whole Hearts.* by Brené Brown
- *Quiet: The Power of Introverts in a World that Can't Stop Talking* by Susan Cain
- *Discovering Your Authentic Core Values: A Step-by-step Guide* by Marc Alan Schelske
- *How Will You Measure Your Life?* by Clayton M. Christensen
- *"What we lost when we stopped reading"* editorial by George Will

LISTEN

- *Happier* with Gretchen Rubin
- *Ten Percent Happier* with Dan Harris by ABC News
- *The Balance Podcast* by BALANCE

WATCH

- *The Bucket List* with Jack Nicholson and Morgan Freeman
- *Wild.* Cheryl Strayed (Reese Witherspoon) makes a decision to halt her downward spiral and put her life back together by hiking the Pacific Crest Trail.
- *My year of saying yes to everything* | Shonda Rhimes—TED Talk
- *What makes a good life? Lessons from the longest study on happiness* | Robert Waldinger—TED Talk

----

ACTION STEPS

Create your own "bucket list" below. What do you want to do, see, visit, read or experience in the next few years and over the course of your life? (Remember, writing these things down dramatically increases the chance they will happen.)

Short-term items:

Long-term items:

Determine what kind of person you want to be? What do you want to stand for? When your life is complete, how do you want to be remembered by others? What do you want them to say about you? After thinking through this, create and list your personal core values that you want to live by throughout your life. Doing this creates guideposts to help you manage the inevitable challenges that will come your way.

Personal core values:

AFTERWORD

My goal in writing this book was to provide a simple "recipe" of sorts for others to dream bigger and to achieve their own unique success in life. It is a resource the reader can come back to again and again as they progress. I learned these concepts from other people and used them throughout my own journey, time and time again. None of the steps are new and they can all be read about and studied in greater detail in many other books. But together they provide a powerful framework for all of us to change, grow and achieve. I hope these steps help you to proactively design and create your own extraordinary life.

I shared many of my personal stories simply to provide real-life examples behind each step. Certainly, there are many people who are much more successful than I am. There are also many who have faced greater challenges and more struggles than I've ever faced. Find out more about these people. Study them. Learn from them. But also know that where there is a will, there is a way. As evidenced from this book, success doesn't just happen. However, neither does failure or stagnation or unhappiness.

No matter where you are today, no matter what obstacles and difficulties you have faced, no matter what negative things people have said about you in the past, you still control what happens in your future. You can achieve your dreams. You have endless opportunities to make your mark on this world. Studying and incorporating these ideas into your own life will make a difference. Just how much of a difference will depend on your personal commitment to do the hard work of vision casting, planning and moving proactively toward your goals.

I wish you a life and career full of meaning and the fulfillment of your biggest dreams. Go out into your future, leverage these ideas and make your life LIMITLESS. You deserve it.

In the end, we only regret the chances we didn't take, the relationships we were afraid to have, and the decisions we waited too long to make.

—LEWIS CARROLL

APPENDIX:
OTHER GREAT RESOURCES

There are so many great resources available for those who want to build a limitless life. Here are just a few additional books that broadly support many of the concepts discussed in this book. Read these as you continue to look for inspiration and tips on your journey to achieve your dreams.

- *The 10X Rule: The Only Difference Between Success and Failure* by Grant Cardone
- *Make Your Bed: Little Things That Can Change Your Life . . . And Maybe The World* by Admiral William H. McRaven
- *The 7 Habits of Highly Effective People: Powerful Lessons in Personal Change* by Stephen R. Covey
- *The Compound Effect . . . Multiplying Your Success One Simple Step at a Time* by Darren Hardy
- *12 Rules for Life* by Jordan B. Peterson
- *Tools of Titans: The Tactics, Routines, and Habits of Billionaires, Icons, and World-Class Performers* by Tim Ferris

ACKNOWLEDGMENTS

Deciding to write a book is not for the faint of heart. All the steps outlined in this book have been important in moving this from an idea in my head to the finished, published product. I used these steps as a constant guide. They do work.

Along the way, there were several champions who helped me get it across the finish line. First, Dawn Pick Benson was my writing partner who helped me put my concepts and ideas into words over lots of meetings, phone calls and drafts. Without her, this never happens. Tim Beals at Credo House Publishers quietly and calmly directed my journey from first draft to published document.

Several friends and colleagues helped push me to complete it as well. Todd Avis, Jim Keane, Jennifer Rumack, John Getgey, John Lame, Chuck Stoddard, Boomer Hoppough, Sarah Brown, Jack VanGessel, Bethany Schutter and Anthony Lazzaro were huge supporters and gave great feedback.

Finally, my wife, Jess, and four kids, Jack, Grace, Pierce and Ben, have had to hear me talk about this for a long time. Their endless support throughout the journey has been remarkable, but I'm sure they are excited to see it end.

To all the above and the many others who helped me along the way, I send a big, heartfelt thanks. You have been wonderful champions for me.

MY LIMITLESS PERSONAL LIFE PLAN

The purpose of this Life Plan is to help you capture key ideas from each chapter and pull them together into one document for easy and regular reference in the future. This is the keystone document that will proactively and subconsciously guide you to your future once it's written down and reviewed regularly.

Name

_____

Date

_____

Commitments I make to "Win the Battle in My Head"

1. _____
2. _____
3. _____

Note: For additional blank versions of this template, go to PeteRuppert.com

Passions and interests I commit to pursue

1. _____

2. _____

3. _____

My long-term vision statement

Clearly lay out details of how I see my extraordinary life 10–25 years from now (personally, professionally and in my family or other relationships)

Champions I will ask to support me on my journey

Note: For additional blank versions of this template, go to PeteRuppert.com

My 3–5 year goals

What will I accomplish in the next five years to build toward my long-term vision?

Professional

Personal/Health

Family/Relationships

Financial

Spiritual

My 1-year goals

Specific goals I will accomplish this year:

Professional

Personal/Health

Family/Relationships

Financial

Spiritual

My first action steps to get the ball rolling (and targeted date of completion)

1. _____

2. _____

3. _____

Note: For additional blank versions of this template, go to PeteRuppert.com

Quarterly check-in goals

What are the next actions I need to take to in the next 90 days to ensure I am on track to accomplish my one-year goals? (Break the one-year goals into smaller increments that you review weekly to ensure you're on track.)

Location where I plan to keep this so I can review it daily

My personal commitment to a limitless life

I promise to believe in myself, find a passion, dream big, take action, be comfortable with failures along the way, show courage and never, ever give up.

Date

_____

My signature of commitment

_____

Note: For additional blank versions of this template, go to PeteRuppert.com

ABOUT THE AUTHOR

Peter Ruppert grew up in Cincinnati, Ohio, as one of six kids with all the typical hopes, dreams, insecurities and fears of most young people. Throughout his youth, his parents emphasized the importance of education. He attended DePauw University in Greencastle, Indiana, where he received his BA in economics. Later, he received his MBA from Harvard Business School. Pete and his wife, Jessica, have four children (Jack, Grace, Pierce and Ben) and reside in East Grand Rapids, Michigan.

Starting in high school, Pete has founded six companies (some of which failed, and all of which provided tremendous learning) and three not-for-profit charitable organizations. He started his career as a sales representative with Procter & Gamble, spent time as a consultant, built his own consulting firm and ran companies for other people. He has been unemployed at least twice.

In 2007, he raised money to launch Fusion Education Group. From a start-up with no revenues, the company has grown to become the leading provider of one-to-one education for middle and high school students throughout the United

States. Today, Fusion Education Group operates more than seventy-five Fusion and Futures Academies in sixteen states and the District of Columbia and recently launched a virtual school, Fusion Global Academy.

Over the past twenty years, Pete has opened more than 120 new schools and acquired more than 25 others. His experience in education spans president and CEO roles in private schools, charter schools and early education. He also served as a public school board member in his local community for five years.

Along Pete's journey toward success, he's studied other successful people and discovered common traits that so many of them exemplified. He wrote this book to provide an easy-to-read and easy-to-use roadmap so that many could benefit.

AUTHOR'S NOTE

I hope this book gets you started on your limitless journey. Please remember that revisiting your plans, updating your vision and setting new goals is a continuous process. Leverage the workbook parts of this whenever possible since they can be a big help.

Also, to share your perspectives, provide feedback, or access more resources, additional blank forms and other *Limitless* tools, please visit *PeteRuppert.com*. I look forward to staying in touch.

All Net proceeds from the sale of Limitless *will go to the Fusion Scholarship Foundation.*